AN ORDINARY
OFFICER'S
UNUSUAL CAREER

AN ORDINARY
OFFICER'S
UNUSUAL CAREER

GEORGE FRANCIS ROWCROFT DSO

edited by DEE STANLEY

AN ORDINARY OFFICER'S UNUSUAL CAREER

Published in 2007 by Dee Stanley
Tregenna, Highcliff Crescent, Seaton, East Devon EX12 2PS

ISBN 978-0-9557691-0-8

Printed by Paperbox
Unit 1 Maida Vale Business Centre, Mead Road, Leckhampton, Cheltenham GL53 7ER
www.paperbox.co.uk

Sir Eric Bertram Rowcroft, CB (1887-1963)

Major General. The first Director of the corp of R.E.M.E.
The barracks at Arborfield is named after him.
His papers and notebooks are held at the R.E.M.E. museum at the REME Museum of Technology,
Isaac Newton Road, Arborfield, Berks, RG2 9NJ.
E-mail:- reme-museum@gtnet.gov.uk
Director Lt. Col (Retd) I.W.J. Cleasby MBE.

Sir Eric was one of George Rowcroft's sons.

Introduction

One day in 1948 an elderly Doctor sat down in a hospital mission and wrote out his life story. He was born in 1861 and rose to be the Colonel of a Sikh regiment. Not so unusual but on his retirement he re-trained as a surgeon and came back into The Indian Army as a Surgeon Major and gave another 40 years of service to the people of the sub-continent.

His journal was handed down the generations until I was fortunate enough to be shown it. I wasn't sure if it would be enjoyed by a wider audience until the typist who put it all onto a "Word disk" told me that she had found it 'fascinating'. This then, is Colonel George Francis Rowcroft's memoirs. As he admits himself, he was no journalist but his little asides as to mundane domestic matters do make interesting reading.

Leaving London on a sombre and grey January day, and arriving in India the next is like walking into a kaleidoscope of vibrant and ever-changing colours. Womens' saris and the exotic array of fruit of every variety displayed on roadside stalls; blue skies and sunshine, and the smells; good mixed in with bad. Good South Indian freshly roasted coffee, its aroma blending in with perfume from the flowers the garland maker is using as he sits cross-legged on the pavement surrounded by yards of freshly strung blossoms threaded onto cotton.

To find Rowcroft's grave I had to motor across the state of Kerala, land of the coconuts, and climb up and into the blue mountains of the Western Ghats. Pioneer Travel of Cochin had provided me with a driver. After filling in umpteen forms at the airport – name rank and number and, for good measure, Father's name as well, I burst out of the exit doors and into a sea of faces, all waiting for someone other than me. Eventually I spotted a card attached to a beaming person. It read 'D. Stanley' and its bearer was Thomas Matthew, my driver and 'oracle' for the next three weeks. Tom was to be my guide on every trip I made to India and in the ensuing years I was drawn back time and time again. Love it or hate it, you cannot ignore India and for those of us who love it then it becomes a drug which has to be taken every year. Tom is a Christian; there are many in Kerala and all of them seem to use the same few names from the Bible. Thomas Matthew or Matthew Thomas, Mark, Luke and John. Our journey was to take us up several thousand feet up into the Western Ghats to that renowned queen of the hill stations, Ootacamunde, Ooty or Snooty Ooty, as the town was known as a resort of the 'posh'. Ooty also has a new Indian name now, this is 'Udagamandalam'. I was to discover that Madras and Bombay and hundreds of other Indian place names have been renamed. The politically correct call them by their new names but most Indians I met do not. Even the newspapers prefer to call Cochin by her old name and not 'Kochi'. Ask a taxi driver for Mahatma Ghandi Road and you will receive blank looks. Ask for M.G. Road and off you go!

The Nilgiri hills are visible at quite a distance and sit on the horizon like brooding bad weather. There is a blue tint about them, which gives the hills their other name, the Blue Mountains. Tom drove me past villages and bazaars and sometimes the road ahead would be strewn with crops that Tom drove over. Peering out of the rear window I asked, "What on earth was that?" Tom replied, "A cheap way of threshing their peas!" Occasionally, Tom needed to ask for directions especially if a road had a detour sign on it. Parking the car safely he would say, "I must go ask for the way, better to be thought a fool than to be a real fool and get lost". I watched as he collared some chap or other. There would then follow an animated conversation between the two of them. Heads would nod and arm gestures would be watched. After a while Tom would come back to the car. I said, "What did he say?" and Tom replied, "I don't know, I didn't understand a word he said." Tom explained, "My language is Malayallam. The next state is Tamil Nadu and everyone speaks Tamil. In the Carnatic they speak Kannadan. Also there is Telagu, Hindi, Urdu and a lot of others." Life here is sometimes confusing.

The Western Ghats begin with a road sign that reads, 'Thirty six hairpin bends'. I should say that really the sign should also add, 'And thirty six heart attacks'. Lorries and buses coming down need to be on our side of the road to negotiate the severe bends in the road. Tom is an experienced and defensive driver and is aware of what to expect and drives accordingly. There are other things on the ever-ascending road to watch out for. Road repair gangs are a constant hazard as they can crop up just anywhere en route. A lorry load of rocks will be dumped on the road and gangs of labourers will be found squatting on the tarmac breaking up rocks with nine-pound lump hammers. On the way, as we go higher, a parapet runs along our nearside. This is to prevent vehicles going over the edge and you really do not want to look over it if you have vertigo. Monkeys sit along the parapet, especially at stopping places. I usually empty the fruit bowls at the last hotel I stayed at for just this purpose. The monkeys are quite adept at catching 'thrown fruit' and I never cease to be fascinated as those tiny fingers peel and segment an orange the same way as we do. Now and again we will arrive at a Chai Stall. This is the ubiquitous hot liquid that begins as tea. By the time it has had condensed milk and concoctions of herbs added to it, it becomes something hot and sweet. It may be very refreshing but it isn't tea! I always carry my own plastic mug as while the 'Tea' is sterilised by heat the cups are rinsed in a bucket of cold and mucky water. As I sat drinking tea on one occasion a pair of crows descended and drank from the washing up bucket. Tom pointed to a flow of water on the offside of the water. "That", he said, "is a clean and fresh natural spring". So I rinsed my cup out in the outflow. Sometimes these small waterfalls will provide the washing facilities for a travelling band of pilgrims on their way to make, 'Puja' at a temple many miles away. Some of their trips can be ten days on the road. A party will hire a minibus and live and eat simply on the way so these waterfalls provide free showers. Eventually we reach the top of the mountain, although deciding where you are is difficult because of the jungle on either side of the road. The checkpoint that covers the road from Kerala and into the state of Tamil Nadu is controlled by a Police Post and once through that your speed drops from an average of thirty mph to five! Beyond the barrier the road as such disappears. It is best described as potholes joined with thin strips of tarmac. The holes can be a foot or more deep and this goes on for miles, all the way to Ooty. I was told that on one visit by a local Government Minister that the angry citizens planted small bushes and banana plants in all the potholes. There were some red faces that day. This part of the journey becomes particularly wearing, especially after seven hours in the car. Happily we arrive in Ooty and bowl into that haven of happiness, The Savoy Hotel. Here the guests are billeted in small bungalows, each consisting of an anteroom, a bedroom and a bathroom. Meals are taken in the dining room and this is an experience not to be missed, especially dinner! As usual, the bar for a pre-dinner drink is a grim place. The staff have to be summoned by bells and often, when the bell does not produce anyone, a trek across the lawns to reception to ask for a barman is necessary. Drinks duly served, the barman disappears again as, seemingly, no one would ever ask for two drinks. I was to find out that in a lot of hotels, the bar is a kind of punishment station. For anyone with the temerity to actually order an alcoholic drink, especially in Hindu India, there are quaint rules about drinking. Various notable Birthdays of Indian 'Saints' will see the shutters on the bar come down with a 'clang'. Best buy a bottle the day before. The entertainment in the dining room at The Savoy is a pianist, a gentleman who wears a flat cap and a cardigan beneath his suit. (It can get chilly at these altitudes). He will beam away at everyone in his vicinity and we will all beam back, not so much from our relaxed and full stomachs and happy dispositions but because he is playing in the style and manner of Les Dawson. The Taj Garden Retreat Hotel at Coonoor stars his protégé on the jo-anna and the bar there is the gloomiest in all of South India.

Coonoor hills, my destination, and Tiger Hill Cemetery is where I discovered the last resting place of George Rowcroft and his family. This was entirely due to the help given me by the British High Commissions Representative for the Nilgiri Hills. Tony Pickford and his wife Bridget have since become great friends of mine. He has secured me interviews with elderly Indians who knew the family and in the case of Benny Raj of Coonoor, in him Tony produced the last servant of the Rowcroft household. Benny keeps the Rowcroft graves tidy and sees that they are litter free and white-washed every year.

Tiger Hills' parent church is 'All Saints', Coonoor. Inside there is a plaque dedicated to George Rowcroft and marking his regular attendance for divine service. It is situated on a pillar going towards the high altar and on the left. At the entrance to the church is a plaque mentioning a General who was assassinated outside in the 1850s'. This little church looks for all the world as if someone had moved it, brick by brick, from the home counties of England.

After my journey to Coonoor and Ooty my UK travel agent, Colours of India, had booked me in what is called a 'Homestay'. This was in the Wyanad district near the small town of Sultans Battery. Tom and I went off on another five-hour jaunt back over those grotty roads until we regained the state of Kerala. Much of the journey was through game parks. I saw monkeys, wild boar and deer. The people behind me in another car saw a tiger! Elephants – wild ones – occasionally step out onto the road (and one did!). Tom said, "They don't seem to like white cars". I made a mental note that our car was white. Tom continued, "I am in reverse gear and I can go backwards very fast". The last advice Tom had was, "And, whatever you do, don't honk the horn at them, they don't like it". The Tusker flapped his ears at us from 50 yards away and then resumed his journey into the forest on the opposite side of the road. Because of this it is advisable to use the bathroom before the journey and do not drink too much at breakfast. Nipping into the forest for a pee can turn into something that could really ruin your day.

Victor Dey runs the Kuppamudi coffee estate at Sultan's Battery and has several rooms that look out onto what must be one of the most beautiful verandas in the world. These are for guests who dine with family and other visitors on communal tables. Each meal becomes an adventure as the conversation moves from guest to guest or to Victor and his family. I never cease to be amazed as complete strangers find out they are related to each other or, at least, they went to the same school. Victor has two Tree Houses for those who would wish to be close to nature. When the squirrels start jumping on the roof at dawn some people decide it is a little too close to nature.

Coffee, unlike tea, is grown in forests. The undergrowth is cleared but most of the mature trees are left standing as Shade Trees. Consequently, the walks around the estate seem like jungle, although the paths are well laid and the direction markers are quite prominent. There are walks uphill to stunning views and shorter routes for the not so fit. Active or not, it's one way to see the real India.

Gini, Victor's wife, must have at least a thousand terra cotta pots full of flowering plants. There is not one patch of soil near the house that does not have a tropical flower in it. The merry song of the Bul-Bul is the first birdsong that will register and then you will see them hopping from one hanging basket to another. Usually these are the Red Vented Bul-Buls and over the years I have been able to identify the Scarlet Minavet and the Racket tailed Drongo. The latter has a long tail with two little feathers at each end so that when it flies it appears as if the Drongo is accompanied by two little birds. There are many others and the Dey library is open to all. This includes books on birds and flora and fauna. I stopped off at Victor's, on my first trip, for two days. Now I stay for at least three weeks, as it is literally paradise on earth. Victor and Gini have a sophistication that is hard to beat in the tourist trade. Daughter Nisha and Son in Law Ajay have also joined the firm now and both of these have the same eager spirit running through their veins.

It is five years since my first trip to India and I shall visit every year until age or funds prohibit my journey. This year is the 150th anniversary of the Indian Mutiny and it seems an appropriate time to publish George Francis Rowcroft's little journal. I cannot but admire him, and his band of men as they stood on that perilous frontier that, still today, takes British lives.

D. Stanley
Tregenna
Seaton, May 2007

Preface

I have not much to add to what I have written in the following story. I could have added much more but it might have wearied the reader.

I hope it will not appear too egotistic, but it only purports to be a narrative of my own life, and something of my experiences.

I have mentioned the names of various Indian places, etc, and I have tried to spell them in the English phonetic way. Those who have lived in India will excuse me.

I find on re-perusal that the literary quality is woefully poor! Paragraphs and incidents in a totally haphazard fashion. Please forgive me! I have not time to write it all over again.

G.F.R.

Thomas Rowcroft 1770 – 1824

Thomas was born illegitimately but cared for by his wealthy uncle in Stroud, Gloucestershire. We took his name from a small plot of land in the town, known as 'Rowcroft'. As soon as he was able he made his way to London and began to better himself. It may well be that his illegitimacy spurred him on to reach for the goal of respectability. He partnered a man called, Rogers in a sailmaking business and financed a venture involving turning copper ingots into tokens. On the military side he raised a troop of volunteer cavalry and became its Commanding Officer. He became a member of The Braziers Guild and a Freeman. After saving some of his wealth he invested in an assurance company and became a director of what was to become The Phoenix Assurance Company. Rumour has it that he travelled to India but I can find no evidence of

this except to say that he was a friend of Francis Rawdon Hastings one time Governor General of India and 1st Marquess of Hastings. Rowcroft acted as an intermediary in the divorce of Queen Caroline and King George The Fourth and supported Hastings in his charitable ventures amongst the poor of Ireland. In later life Hastings became rather broke and I wonder if Thomas Rowcroft loaned him money. However, Thomas had his eye on a Government job and after beseeching Parliament to employ him as an Ambassador he was given the post of our first consul to the newly emerging country of Peru. An old adage says, "Be careful what you wish for". In Thomas' case it was aptly true for after sailing to Peru with his daughter and beginning his task as Consul he was accidentally shot by one of Simon Bolivars soldiers. Boliver, himself was aghast at what had happened and personally met Miss Rowcroft. On her route home she married the Captain of the British Warship conveying her to England. On an amusing note I found that Thomas wrote copiously and forwarded reports back to England rather more often than the official in charge of receiving such reports would deem necessary. The official wrote to Rowcroft reproving him about this and as an added remonstration suggested that Rowcroft, "use no more of the hand currently employed in writing such reports". In other words, his handwriting was abysmal.

Francis Rawdon Rowcroft 1802 – 1877
Lt General, CB, Indian Army.

Obviously the General's middle name was given to him because of the connection his father had with The Marquess of Hastings.

During the Indian Mutiny Rowcroft was promoted from Colonel to Brigadier and given the Sarun Field Force to command. This group included The Royal Naval landing party from HMS Pearl.

Two writers have mentioned that Brigadier Rowcroft was a cautious Commander and said it in an insulting manner. I must point out that Rowcroft won all his battles despite being heavily outnumbered and was careful with the lives of his men.

Whilst his three sons were young he rented a house in Kimbolton Avenue in Bedford and sent them to Bedford School. Another young man at the school was Revely Mitford. His mother took tea with Mrs Rowcroft in the avenue. Mrs Mitford's husband died whilst they were in India and she re-married her childhood sweetheart, William Hodson, the man who founded Hodson's Horse and who shot dead the sons of the last Moghul King of Delhi.

Lt. General Rowcroft retired to Torquay and died in 1877.

George Cleland Rowcroft 1831 – 1922
Major General, Indian Army.

Bedford School in the 1840's. I have a copy of the school register which shows him and his brother, 'Fred' attending the school as Dayboys. George was sent to India in 1849 from Portsmouth on the East India Company's ship, Alfred. The journey took six months. Whilst a young man he wrote an article or two on the subject of the North West Frontier and the best anyone could expect would be death arriving quickly in the shape of a bullet, and the worst was the unspeakable torture inflicted on a wounded and helpless soldier caught alone in those cruel hills. 2007, and nothing seems to have changed much.

We tend to lose track of George until much later in his life, I know he served in the Indian Mutiny in 1857-8 and I have his medal beside me as I write.

George Cleland Rowcroft
Major General, Indian Army
George Francis' Father

In 2002 I found a book on the Mutiny in a second hand book shop in Lyme Regis. In the margins George had written much on his experiences in India at that time. He talks of living with Hodson and his wife at their bungalow in Kussowlie and on one notable page he writes how he dragged a muddy Subaltern called Roberts out from beneath his horse after he fell into a ditch. The Roberts he mentions became Field Marshall, The Earl Roberts, V.C., of Kandahar. He proposed that Rowcroft become a Mason and he was duly enrolled in the Freemasons Lodge called Khyber! In old age, Major General Rowcroft seems to have become a Martinet. His photograph showing him in civilian clothes depicts a man who stands proudly before the camera. The family tell me that he could be 'difficult'.

Francis Rowcroft, died 1883.

Colonel 4th Prince of Wales Gurkha Regiment. 'Fred', to the rest of the family.

His photograph shows him as a robust powerfully built man, fairly tall with a dark moustache. He was also a pupil at Bedford School and he and his brother George married two girls known as the Souper sisters. Their father was Registrar General of Mauritius. His name was P. Souper!!

Fred took his gallant band of Gurkhas on Roberts' famous march from Kabul to Kandahar. He features in the wounded lists of that time but his injury is called, slight. I only know from his letters that this period of service coming so late in his career was particularly onerous and seems to have had an effect on his general health. He retired to Brighton in 1883 and the first winter with its crop of the usual coughs, colds and influenza seems to have caused Fred's unfortunate demise. All he had to show for a lifetime of duty in India was a bequest to his wife of £200.00 pounds. Others went to make their fortunes but

Fred Rowcroft came home broken in health. One of his sons became an academic and married an heiress to the Wills Tobacco fortune – they settled in Torquay and due to Mrs Rowcroft's (nee Wills) generosity to the town there is a road, a hospital ward and a hospice named Rowcroft.

George Francis Rowcroft DSO, 1861-1953.
Colonel 15th Ludihana Sikhs.
The subject of this book.

Sir Eric Bertram Rowcroft, CB 1887 – 1963.
Major General. The first Director of The Corp of R.E.M.E.
Sir Eric is well researched. Rowcroft Barracks at Arborfield is named for him and his papers and notebooks are held by the REME Museum.
He retired to Lyme Regis in Dorset.

Maurice George Rowcroft, 1887-1974.
Lt Colonel. Indian Army Service Corps.

I came upon Maurice's' last resting place in Tiger Hill cemetery, Coonoor, Nilgiri Hills, South India in 2003. No grave marker but a plain mound of soil. Maurice was the last of The Indian Rowcrofts. Whilst he had buried his parents and sister, there was no one to provide a gravestone for him. By the time of my next visit in 2004 he had been provided with a black marble stone. It was then that The Urban Co-operative Bank of Coonoor approached me and said, "Can we add something to the gravestone?" It was: - President of Bank 1959-1970. Maurice became a bank clerk in Canada during one of his fathers' adventures in that land.

When the Great War broke out in 1914 Maurice enlisted in a Canadian Regiment. Once back in England he transferred to The Lincolnshire Regiment. He was instrumental in saving a Sergeants life who was buried by an explosion. Maurice, despite a severe wound in his leg, helped dig the Sergeant out, before seeking treatment himself at the hospital tents. After the war Maurice joined the Indian Arms Service Corp. There are stories of him in the Second World War striding about, waving his walking stick and urging his men to make greater efforts for the war. Maurice, it seems, was a popular fellow.

In later life he rented rooms at his club and other retired Colonels rented rooms close by. I should have loved to eavesdrop on conversations at dinner. A

Colonel Mathieson requested that when Rowcroft died he be buried close by. I discovered Mathieson's grave by Rowcroft's.

Friends in death as well as life. A fortunate man.

In the photographs I have of Maurice, he leans heavily on a stick and his leg is bent inwards. He must have carried that pain since 1916 but rarely mentioned it.

There are other Rowcrofts. One was a Colonel of Hodson's Horse and another founded Geelong Grammar School in Australia – as attended by The Prince of Wales. One got up to no good in Cincinnati, America, and seems to have been run out of town. The majority were the reliable 'duty men' of history.

Dedication

I first met Dee Stanley subsequent to an enquiry at my office here in Wellington, Tamil Nadu, South India.

As the British Deputy High Commissions representative for this very mountainous area covering some 800 square miles I receive many requests involving British residents, as people attempt to trace their ancestors. I find that most enquiries involve the deceased. The number of people who have forebears here is massive and these enquiries increase every year. Dee wanted to know about the Rowcroft family who lived here years ago and are buried at Tiger Hill cemetery in Coonoor. Did their graves exist? What state were they in? - and any other information I could gleam from those still alive who remembered them.

I had heard of the Rowcrofts, who were much respected, but this is Dee's story and she is far more qualified than I to tell you about George Rowcroft and his family.

I arranged to meet her at Tiger Hill cemetery, she was early, as she always is and delighted to finally pause at the grave of George Francis Rowcroft, DSO, a man she had been researching for a very long time. This, for her, was journey's end, and a trip of several thousand miles.

The graves of Rowcroft and his family were in a poor condition and Dee immediately organised a fighting fund to repair all the headstones, and in Maurice Rowcroft's case, provide a dark slab of polished Rajastan marble as he had no epitaph until then. She kindly deputised me to hold the money and to oversee the work. Later she involved The British Association for Cemeteries South Asia (BACSA) to provide funds for repairing the wall and gatehouse.

It has been a pleasure and a privilege for me and myself to become close friends with Dee and Jim, her long suffering partner, for a number of years now. We always meet up on her annual visits as we enjoy the wonderful stories she tells with such whacky humour; the lady is unique but that aside 'she knows her subject'. Those of you who read George's journal will find it hugely interesting.

Your friend in the hills of South India.
Tony Pickford
Wellington, Coonoor, South India

Many thanks to the following:
> Michael Goodliff, a Rowcroft without whose help I should have been lost.
> BACSA – British Association for Cemeteries South Asia.
> E-mail: bacsamember@aol.com
> Colours of India, Travel Agents
> Partnership Travel Ltd, Marlborough House, 298 Regents Park Road, London N3 2TJ
> Pioneer Travel of Cochin, India
> Pioneer House, 5th Cross Road, Willingdon Island, Cochin, Kerala, South India
> E-mail: pioneer@pner.com
> Victor & Gini Dey
> Luxury Holidays. E-mail: homestay@vsnl.com
> Thomas Matthew – Driver
> Jim Featherstone – Burra Sahib!

AN ORDINARY OFFICER'S UNUSUAL CAREER

by GEORGE FRANCIS ROWCROFT DSO
Colonel 15th Ludihana Sikh Regiment and
latterly Surgeon Major, Indian Army

edited by DEE STANLEY

For
Stella, of The Bexhill Hanoverians

My grandfather and father were both in the Indian Army, I and my youngest brother followed suit. My second brother would probably have done the same, but unhappily went blind from ophthalmia in India when quite an infant. Both grandfather and father were in the Indian Mutiny of 1857/8 and the former had a wonderful escape once. Riding under the branch of a tree he bent his head to avoid it and at that instant a cannon ball hit and broke the branch; shouts from nearby soldiers cried 'the Brigadier's killed!'. However, the Brigadier bobbed up smiling, having sustained no injury.

The two earliest things I can remember were while going home from India at the age of two, in 1863, and getting a sweet stuck in my throat while on deck. Someone, possibly the ship's Doctor upended me and shook me up and down on the top step of a companionway leading down to the saloon. I remember at the time my chief fear was that I should be shot down the stairs!

Presumably, the sweet was dislodged.

The other event was a shark being caught and dragged along the deck. A little Scots Terrier ran along side yakking at the shark; unfortunately the shark wasn't done for, and managed to nip the dog, which sent it on its way.

Years afterwards I was told by my mother there was a certain army Captain on board who took a shine to me and told my mother that out of all the children on board I was the only one he would jump overboard for if I fell in. I only mentioned this because years afterwards I was appointed to the Dorset Regiment, and he was the Commanding Officer; obviously neither of us recognized each other. It is funny what you remember when you are tiny, but I do recall a marvellous display of shooting stars on the 16 November 1866, whilst living with my grandparents at Holcombe in Devonshire. Grandfather was Lieutenant General, Francis Rawdon Rowcroft, C.B. - the very Brigadier who had led the Sarun Field Force and the men of HMS Pearl's Naval Brigade. I do recall we had a very kind nurse whom we loved very much. She told me that she was leaving us the next day and would be starting so early we shouldn't be up to say goodbye. I decided otherwise. It was when I arose at some unearthly hour, more than likely 4.00am and looked out of the window up to the night sky. The stars appeared to have gone mad, there were scores of them piercing the sky in every direction. I assumed in my innocence that this was the normal heavenly state of affairs, and so I didn't wake anyone else up. Later they told me they would have given their eye teeth to have seen that display. That was my compensation as I then overslept and missed the departure of my nurse.

THOMAS ROWCROFT
Cartoon from the 1820's

Our first consul to Lima - Peru. Accidentally shot and killed by one of Bolivars Sentries in 1824.

Soon afterwards we moved to France for five years. We had a house at Avranches, where much fighting took place in the Great War. We lived next to a nice French protestant couple whose name escapes me. The husband was an Officer in the Gendarmes, who used to smoke cigars, exciting my youthful admiration. Just outside our kitchen door was a grapevine with several nice bunches on it, the lowest one easily within my reach, which my mother forbade me to touch. I am afraid I was quite a little beast (and I am afraid I am now an older one). One morning when mother was out, I picked the bunch and ate every one, and very good they were too. To complete my enjoyment, M'seur Massigne (I have just remembered his name, although I am not sure of the spelling) had lit a cigar and after a few puffs had thrown it away. I picked it up and smoked it with great joy, and just afterwards my mother came in. She at once noticed that the bunch of grapes had disappeared. Did I know what had happened to it? I knew nothing about it, I lied. Then I complained of feeling ill, and then I was very ill, and my mother soon knew where the grapes had gone. I deserved a good hiding, but she was too kind to administer one.

In 1870, the Franco-Prussian War broke out. The winter was an extremely cold one. French troops were in camp in the vicinity and I remember being told one morning that 13 French soldiers had been frozen to death the previous night.

On Saturday afternoons all the British residents used to meet at a Municipal building and make bandages from clean tablecloths and sheets to provide some medical assistance for the French wounded. I would like to mention something, which I have never seen referred to in any book, but as I saw it with my own eyes it may well have had something to do with the final debacle at Sedan. The Garde Mobile used to drill in their thousands in the local area, and I saw them loading their old muzzle-loaders. To do this, a man had to be standing, draw his ramrod and after putting in the powder, wad and musket ball, ram down hard and put his ramrod back in its casing. He could then lie or kneel in order to shoot. All this time he would be facing the Germans with their modern breechloaders. These men, we were told, were sent to Sedan, and I know some, who had been workmen on our house, who became casualties there, presumably from having to face a modern army, with antique weapons.

After that we came to England, and I was sent to a private school. I don't think I cared for the lessons much. We took Latin and Greek. I spent most of my time staring out of the window, or doing something that I shouldn't, like taking my watch to pieces. After that I was sent to Bradfield. Every week a list would be posted up of our performance in lessons, the marks being shown in Greek letters. Each letter meant something, and I never quite understood what, but certain letters meant that the next morning you went to the Headmaster's study for a sound thrashing, which I knew to be quite severe, as the boys who had been punished used to display their anatomy to their classmates. I never knew whether I was in for a whacking; I suppose it kept me on my toes because in all my time at Bradfield I was never birched. The Masters were allowed to cane us on the palms of our hands, and I got my fair share of that. I wonder one's fingers and hands were not permanently damaged, as the cane was quite savagely administered at times. We used to play tricks on the French Master, though he turned the tables on us:- it was winter so there was a fire in the classroom grate. About a quarter of an hour before the lesson began a boy produced a frying pan and filled it with red-hot coals and then applied chilli powder and ran about the room filling it with suffocating smoke (one should try the experiment - I will guarantee satisfaction!). When he could bear it no longer he put it down, and we all mustered outside in the corridor and the frying pan was hidden away. When the French Master came along we told him something had happened and no one could go into the room. He put his nose in at the door and said 'Well, I think you had all better go in and I'll stay out here', and in we had to go. We frantically opened every window, but with smarting and streaming eyes and noses we vowed never to repeat the experiment.

From Bradfield I went to Cheltenham College. It had an excellent gymnasium, and I used to spend a lot of my spare time exercising. We also had two French Masters, one of whom wore spectacles. Whenever I misbehaved in class, and he had his back to me, he always told me what I had done. At first I could not understand how he had eyes in the back of his head, but then I realized that on the outer edge of his spectacles and with the blackboard in front of him, he had the perfect mirror image of my evil little ways. I was not an ace at mathematics and I told my parents that I did not think I would do well enough for the army exam. I loathed the subject. I was sent to a crammer. A charming man - Mr James - taught me mathematics, and in three months I was proficient at the subject. We had a big old house at the time, and if I was studying late at night whilst everyone else had gone to bed I would imagine all sorts of eerie noises, and the house creaked as the warmth of the sun during the day had caused the timbers to expand, and now during the night-time they contracted, making their creaking noises. From beneath me one evening I heard a sound like a ghostly drummer and went down into the scullery to find that the clothes horse had fallen against the wall and its legs juddered against the stone floor. This was the noise I'd heard in the room above, which sounded just like a phantom drummer. As children we all play at being ghosties, but many absolutely trustworthy folks will testify on a stack of bibles that certain houses are haunted. I suppose there is hardly a single family who cannot produce a member who has not seen, or alleged to have seen, a spook. Personally, I have had only one experience.
I was about ten years of age, and my mother and I were staying at the time with my Aunt at Rock Ferry near Birkenhead. She had three French gentlemen as paying guests. I must describe how the rooms at one end of the first floor were

situated. On the left was a door leading into my mother's room and at right angles to this a passage with first a small narrow room, which was mine, then one of the Frenchmen's. Sometime after having gone to bed late, I realised that I had no matches and so I went to ask my mother for some. I left my door open, went into mother's room and in the dark I went to wake her. My wrist was suddenly grabbed and an agitated voice called out, 'Who's there?' I had entered the Frenchman's room by mistake. He lit a match and showed me to the door, I thanked him and apologised and was left once more in the pitch dark. I then began to hear the sound of heavy breathing coming from where, I didn't quite know. Realising that I had better cut my losses I thought I had better return to my own bed, and then realised that the breathing was coming from my bedroom. I rationalised that some poor tired soul in desperate need of sleep had occupied one half of my bed in the short period that I was out of it, and I must do my best not to disturb them. Of course, when I awoke in the morning there was absolutely nothing there!

The only other scrap of note that I can recall in childhood was that my brother and I acquired an old cannon - with a half-inch bore - mounted on a solid wooden block. We loaded some lead into it, having primed it with some black powder, and fired it. There was a crash of broken glass and shouts rented the air! We thought: 'Hello?', re-loaded and fired once more - more broken glass and shouts!
It then occurred to us that possibly there was some connection between our firing the cannon and the shouting. I went to investigate and sure enough we had shot through a large frosted window in a house opposite, which happened to be occupied by some plumbers. Fortunately, none of them were injured. I recall there was an exchange of coin of the realm, and we stopped firing, and the incident was quietly closed.

Goodbye England

In due time I passed into and out of Sandhurst Military College, and was gazetted into the 54th Foot, 2nd Battalion Dorset Regiment, and I received orders to join them in Burma. Shortly before sailing the family moved to Weston-Super-Mare which, I thought, was a horrible place. The advertisements on railway station hoardings pictured it with blue seas and extensive golden sands. In reality, the tide goes out for miles, leaving acres and acres of liquid mud, and the water - when the tide was in - was a muddy brown. There were no sands at all! I sailed on the 29th September 1879 on one of the older troop ships, the Euphrates. For the first two or three days I was horribly seasick, but found my sea legs after a short while. The day before we sailed I saw a peculiar phenomenon. That afternoon on the 28th September there was a strange white halo around the sun. Crossing this at right angles was another immense white halo; on either side of the sun there were two bright patches almost like mirror images of the sun. I have not seen them before, or since, and they did not appear to herald any particular good or really bad weather. (Editor's note: some people call this strange light around the sun Fire Dogs, and my uncle, working as a farmhand on the great plains of America saw this occurrence many times.).

Delhi and Meerut

We reach Bombay in about a month (Editor's note: The SS Euphrates gained India via the Suez Canal. It is interesting to note, George's father in 1849 took six months to reach the same destination. This was obviously prior to the construction of the Canal). There were three other Subalterns who had been posted with me to the 54th and one of them landed ashore with me in a barge with a Major. As we stepped ashore, the Major's brother met him, and was so overcome with delight that he asked the whole of us, complete strangers to him, to dinner at a large club. I thought to myself 'Well this is a fine start to my life in India'. We actually had quite a first rate dinner too. Landing into the surf was quite a hairy experience, and the two Indian boatman in charge of the baggage began to argue with one another as to who was to take my luggage ashore and between them they dropped my portmanteau which held my uniform clothing and other gear into the sea! Fortunately, it was at once seized and pulled back into the boat. It was a brand new chest and the lid must have fitted rather well for when I opened it, expecting to find my clothing soaked, it was all perfectly dry.

The three things, which struck me first in India:
1.   Was the boldness of the crows. (Editor's note: George seemed to have a thing about crows, and as this journal continues it is a subject he will return to time and time again).
2.   The excellence and good repair of the roads. (Editor's note: I hate to say this, as I love India dearly, but some of the roads I have travelled recently would not have been awarded George's approbation).
3.   The way that all or most of the trees bore pretty coloured flowers.

My father at this time was commanding his Indian Regiment at Allahabad and let me know that during my voyage out, the 54th HQ had returned from Burma to India and were at Delhi, so I was directed to report there. I managed to get 10 days leave and stayed with my father at Allahabad, and then reported to Delhi. The Regiment had been in India a good many years. (Editor's note: The

Regimental badge of the Dorsets depicts the works, Primus in Indus). In the ranks there were about 300 seasoned old stagers with at least 21 years' service. It was due to leave for England in about two years but for some reason the War Office directed it to stay in India. (Editor's note: At about this time the Zulu War had occupied British troops in South Africa and another of Queen Victoria's little wars was brewing in the Middle East). One of the Sergeants whom I liked well was so disappointed at being required to remain in India that he shot himself, but only managed to blow off half his face, and in his agony finished off the task by cutting his own throat. We were quartered in the fort, and us Subalterns had to live in the Nobat Khana, which I heard was the old theatre of the Kings of Delhi. (Editor's note: George's father in 1840 marched up country, had a piece of land pointed out to him in the jungle, and was required to build his own accommodation). In the hot weather the temperature in my room regularly reached 107 degrees. The river Jumna was quite near and in the monsoon, the water came right up to the fort walls and I could fish directly from my window. I remained empty handed, or fishless but a companion caught a large turtle. It was quickly killed and its stomach cut open to reveal a half digested puppy, a water rat and the brown forearm of a baby, presumably bitten off a dead infant. As I say, these turtles were quite large. Once I was shooting and wading through shallow water when I found myself being transported along. I had stepped on the back of a turtle, which had been lying doggo at the bottom.

There was plenty of shooting around about Delhi. Wild fowl of all sorts and black buck. I was told about something that had happened prior to my arrival when one of the Officers who was a good shot went out after black buck. He was unsuccessful, and on the way home, crossing some ploughed fields, he saw a white crockery pot. Indian farmers place these upturned pitchers on sticks in the fields as a type of scarecrow and these are quite effective at deterring birds scavenging on newly planted crops. Our marksman decided on some target practice and at some distance fired three times at the pot and missed. He then received the shock of his life as a sleeping Indian awoke and slowly and calmly walked away.

Our hunter had been shooting at the white pugree, which the man was wearing on his head.

From Delhi, the 54th marched to Meerut (Editor's note: Meerut is approximately 30 miles from Delhi and a march of that distance in those days, which did not have any urgency about it would have taken about two to three days). A few days after arriving we dined with the Officers of the Durham Light Infantry. Bottles of brandy were produced which I discovered had been hidden away by the old Mess Bearer during the Indian Mutiny of 1857, and had been maturing ever since. It was supposed to be super-excellent and was passed around as a liqueur. I tasted a little, but (not an expert at my age) I couldn't tell if it were vintage or not. (Editor's note: On the evening of May 10th 1857, the Church bells sounded their call to prayer across the cantonment at Meerut, and it was there that the Mutiny proper burst into flames).

I was plagued by mosquitoes at Meerut - especially during the rains. I counted 26 sat on my toothbrush one day. The hot weather was unbearable and I recall after a shower of rain, the savage heat suddenly dropped down to 90 degrees in the Mess. This was such a sudden drop in temperature I searched about for a coat to put on.

I continued my duties as a newly arrived young Officer and not without mishap. As orderly Officer I had the key of the Regimental cash chest. The key should have been on one of those huge fobs that they give you in hotels in order that you do not depart with it, however, the small fobless key that I had escaped from the small hole in my trouser pocket. I was not popular. It took the Armourer the best part of two days working with a hacksaw, a hammer, and a cold chisel to break the chest open, and I was presented with a nice little bill to pay for it.

In the heavy rain of the wet weather, monsoon ditches took surplus water away from the Cantonment. Such was the rush of water after a cloudburst, people and animals were sometimes carried away and drowned and so one had to be careful to avoid falling into these ditches. (Editor's note: It was fairly common for drunken soldiers to fall in a dry ditch and continue to sleep off the effects of the alcohol and in the rains the ditches filled rather quickly and the man was drowned. Nowadays they are concrete lined and six feet deep and once in there is no way out).

Funny things at Roorke

At the end of 1880 we marched to Roorke. There was a forest called the Puttree and it was reputed to be full of game. One of our Officers went into the forest to shoot. He heard the call of a spotted deer and discovered it had been seized by a python, which was coiled around it, squeezing the deer to death. He shot the python and the deer struggled out and made off at a speed which showed it to be unhurt. I am now 86 years of age, and I have had many experiences whilst out shooting, and someone up there must like me as I nearly came a cropper on more than one occasion. One day I was in a large pond and had shot several birds that waded in to retrieve. The lake was full of dense weed and I had to force my way through it. If I had lost my footing I should have been hopelessly entangled and drowned as has happened to many a sportsman. The bottom shelved steeply and first I was up to my knees, then my thighs, waist and chest. Finally I was up to my neck in it, literally! I had put my cartridges into my hat to keep them dry. Finally the water was up to my mouth and not yet having reached the birds I had shot, I had to turn with difficulty and wade out again covered in green slime.

Animal life was plentiful, especially during the rainy season. My wooden tub in the bathhouse used to be a haven for frogs and on one occasion I shared my bath with 57 of them jumping around me while I was bathing. The local white ants - when they were ranging around for new territory, used to build themselves little mud tunnels up walls and across ceilings. On this occasion they made a tunnel up the outside of my bath and on coming out of it at the top began to commence operations on my back. When putting one's boots on I discovered a fat toad in one of them, and on donning my coat, a fat hairy rat shot out of the sleeve. Snakes were also a problem. I would take my company down to the rifle ranges in the cool of the early morning accompanied by my Colour Sergeant. He would dismiss the men until such times as the Superintending Officer rode down and practice could begin. The men were amusing themselves as usual and one of them saw a snake entering a hole in the field embankment. He seized it by the tail and pulled it out and then began whirling it around his head to prevent it biting him. Then it occurred to him that if he stopped this action the snake might bite him, so he didn't know what to do but to continue waving this snake around in a wild fashion. One of the old sweats casually suggested quietly that he really ought to fling it away. This had not occurred to the snake man, and with a smile of relief he quickly got rid of it by throwing it from him as far as he possibly could. At the end of the shoot I had to go down to the butts to count

"Cutting a Dash" Colonel G. Rowcroft wearing a blazer. Peshawar - April 1902

and check the scores on the targets. As this was some hundreds of yards away I galloped the distance on my horse. Across the range was a rather wide ditch and my horse tripped on a tussock of grass and pitched me off it. The second I hit the ground my first thought was to roll away fast in case the horse fell on me. I managed a quick look over my shoulder and saw the horse standing clean on his head, all four legs in the air, and tail pointing skywards before crashing to the ground and landing in the exact spot that I had just rolled away from. The Major ran up to me looking quite concerned as he thought I had been killed, but riding accidents were all part of the hazards of the job.

Riding out with a brother Officer we reached a tiny streamlet some few feet wide with just a little water in it. My companion was leading and walked into what seemed to him to be a shallow streambed. To my astonishment the horse plunged into liquid mud up to its neck. My companion dismounted in an undignified manner whilst I just sat there and laughed at him. He was not best pleased. To avoid that spot I moved upstream further and crossed at a safer place, and exactly the same thing happened to me. Down into the mud went my horse, taking me with it. Needless to say, my companion became hysterical with joy and didn't stop laughing for hours.

Our daily guards were mounted near the corner of one of the barrack rooms. One evening I happened to be passing the spot and although no guard was there I heard all the words of command associated with the guard, being loudly and clearly given. Was I dreaming? I looked about and found a large grey parrot in a cage nearby. Obviously he had picked up the routine and his voice was word perfect and very Sergeant Major-like. These things are all part of the warp and weft of life.

During the hot weather I had taken my chair outside of the mess one evening and placed it on the grass. Joy of joys! - I had obtained a newly-arrived newspaper. I had just finished reading about the murder of Czar Alexander in Russia by a bomb, when a bomb went off right behind me. Or so it seemed. I leapt out of my chair and discovered that behind me there were two large earthenware jars about two feet across and full of water. A dozen bottles of soda water had been put into one of the jars to cool. Something had happened to explode them and the whole lot went off at once, with the result that I gave this method of cooling beverages considerable respect and a very wide berth in the future.

On one of my duties I was ordered to march a party of fifty invalids and convalescents to Landour - the military station of Mussoorie - in the Himalayas, about five or six marches off. (Editor's note: one march equals one day, usually conducted in the cool of the morning at 4 or 5am when the men would strike camp and march in the day until 9 or 10.00am when they would pitch camp and relax for the rest of the day). I wasn't warned or told what arrangements to make for my own requirements, and being green went to the march without any food. I assumed the Indian contractor who provided the mens' rations would provide mine. Not a bit of it! He had no spare food for me.

At the end of the trip I was as near starved as I have ever been but I had learned another lesson the hard way.

My regiment was quite wealthy, and considered a smart one to be in. We had a large gold dinner service used at every guest night, and all in all, not having private means, I decided I would be better off in the better paid Indian Army, and so after my compulsory two years' service with the Dorsets I had the good fortune to be posted to the 15th Ludihana Sikh Regiment, then stationed at Delhi.

With the 15th Sikhs

I liked being back in Delhi.

There was much to enjoy and many diversions, although it did have some drawbacks. The place seemed to abound with snakes, the River Jumna, as I have said before, used to overflow and I saw five cobras swimming together. An old Indian used to fish them out and put them in earthenware pots. He used to empty them out one by one and show them to us for a small reward. I noticed that he was missing a thumb and that in his belt he carried an axe. He told us that a snake had bitten him on the thumb, but before the poison could circulate he had cut off the thumb and saved his life.

Delhi also had scorpions.

One evening, bathing before dinner in the dark, I left the kerosene lamp in my room with the door ajar to give me some light. After my bath, I slipped one foot into a shoe and felt something moving, so took my foot out again and there sat on my toes was a fair sized scorpion. Believe me - I shook it off fast! Scorpions sting from the tail and can cause death. In future I learned not to stick my feet into what could be a dark retreat for something nasty!

Other entertainments are jugglers and they are very clever. I saw some really entertaining stuff. One of the jugglers asked for a reel of cotton, which was duly provided for him by one of our mess servants. The juggler pulled off several yards of cotton, rolled it up and swallowed it. His only clothing was a loincloth. He produced a penknife and cut a small nick in the skin just below his ribs. He picked away at this spot and seemingly got hold of the end of a thread and began to pull it out of his body hand over hand. The first two or three inches were blood stained but the rest of it was quite clean, he then broke the thread leaving four or five inches still hanging out. I tried to get hold of the broken end but he would not let me touch it. He then began to pat his stomach an inch or two away from the thread. At each pat the thread retreated within him until it disappeared.

Now, I ask you, how on earth did he work that one?!

Another trick he performed that night was to take a fairly thick piece of bamboo, about the diameter of a glass tumbler. This was cut off at a joint so that it would indeed carry water. He showed us that it was perfectly empty and poured a handful of sand into it. He called one of the mess servants over and asked him to hold out his hand and he then tipped the bamboo into the palm of his hand, when he removed the cup the man was holding three large scorpions which he dropped like red hot rivets.

Delhi Fort was overrun with squirrels. These are much smaller than their English cousins, have a stripe down their backs and resemble the American chipmunks. My brother-in-law was accompanied by his two English terriers and they loved chasing squirrels but never caught them as they usually shinned up the nearest tree. On this occasion a crow had seen the squirrels escape and had seized one in its beak and threw it down to the dogs who quickly killed it - now you know why I don't like crows.

The local people, especially the villagers in the area and surrounding district, were incredibly friendly, but now, alas, I am afraid it is not so, for which we must thank the politicians and their hangers-on.

At about this time I found myself Quarter Master of the Regiment. We were not regulation bound in those days and Commanding Officers were allowed a little initiative. Our regulations consisted of a small book about a half-inch thick, and named 'Standing Orders for the Bengal Infantry', and a few small books on Pay, Clothing and Transport. And everything went swimmingly. The Quarter Master used to be allowed 25 Rupees a month to keep the tents repaired. Once they were absolutely beyond repair a Committee condemned them and new ones were ordered. This was all changed later for a mass of paperwork and trouble and a great worry to everyone concerned.

And of course, the costs trebled.

Part of my duty was to learn the local language and I had to study under an Indian linguist usually called a Munshi. Escaping my studies I decided to go to the zoo. I shouldn't have really because my language exams were due. I was admiring a chameleon in a glass case. The only other people nearby were a lady and gentleman. The building was open at the sides, the roof being supported by columns. There was an explosion and a ball of fire seemed to come from

Group of 15th Sikh Officers and Ladies

outside like a molten cricket ball. It streaked through the air and hit the glass case that contained the chameleon. The lady nearby shrieked and threw her arms around the gentleman's neck, the plate glass of the tank was riven and the animal inside had disappeared. Outside, a palm tree was smoking and burnt black. I went back to the glass case and there was the chameleon again. It must have changed colour in shock and thus I had not been able to see it after the explosion. We discussed the matter and it seems that ball-lightening must have been responsible.

Insects and other creepy crawlies

Do you want to see insects? Go to Delhi during the rains.

In the evening when the lamps are lit insects come round in their millions and swarm into the rooms. An entomologist could make a good collection in one evening. I collected butterflies, moths and beetles. Flying bugs were the most numerous and were an absolute pest. They used to fall into everything, including meals. Feeding became an art, especially if you were eating soup. Many was the time I have had to fish out a beetle or two doing the backstroke in my brown Windsor soup. We used to play billiards after dinner. The table used to look as if it had been peppered with insects. One of us would stand by with a clothes brush. A player would be asked to nominate which ball he was aiming at and then a path would be brushed from the cue ball to the target.

During the hot weather I obtained a short leave and went to Mussoorie in the hills. Altitude meant the weather was cooler and I was very grateful. I went with a party to a picnic at a beauty spot called the Mossy Falls. It was, sadly, noted for leeches so I put on Wellington boots under my trousers. When I got back to my bungalow I found lots of blood inside my boots, and had three bites on one leg and two on the other. On returning to Delhi these bites used to irritate most maddeningly, until after a few months they turned into what we called Delhi Sores. They would not heal, so I was given ten days leave to Patiala, which did the trick. The British Resident there put me up and we were close to the palace of the State Rajah. I was invited to see his private collection of guns and rifles; there were hundreds of them! I was also shown his museum. This was an eclectic array of unusual objects. He had a number of single and double brass bedsteads. He also had a room devoted to camping equipment, most of which was contained in a variety of portable bags. Every kind of camp past-time was catered for, even down to painting and watercolour sets.

Once a year we had to carry out field firing. This was mock attacks on prepared positions representing an enemy line with small targets dotted about. On reaching my designated position we were allowed to fall out, and await the General's arrival. The ground in front was fairly open and in the distance, I could see some village pigs routing about. A brother officer took a look and said, 'Those are wild pigs', and with that he and I jumped on our horses and galloped towards them. I began to think; if we do come up on them what on earth are we going to kill them with? Normally this game is pursued with spears, although we did have our swords with us. We went after big boar, which took cover in some elephant grass. Taking a side each we patrolled the perimeter hoping to flush it out. Presently there was a loud grunt and out dashed the boar at my horse. He came at such an awkward angle that I missed him with my sword, and in passing he gave my horse a slight cut in the flank with his tusk and made good his escape, and we returned to that which we should have been doing in the first place, namely our mock battle.

Malaria and Medals

From time to time surveys are carried out around army cantonments, sometimes by parties of Officers and sometimes by a single Officer. I have done both.

Three of us were sent out from Delhi on a survey. We sent a man in every day for food. Our bread was pretty tasteless and always white so when he presented us with a brown loaf we were quite surprised. On cutting it open we saw a large patch in the centre was snow white. I had a word with the messenger and he casually informed me that on the way out he had dropped it in a muddy puddle, but managed to dry it in the sun before handing it over. I don't recommend this method for making wholemeal loaves. Despite this I had managed, so far, to remain fit, but getting out of bed the next day I suddenly collapsed. Within a minute or two I felt fine and after washing and dressing I presented myself at breakfast, mentioning my collapse to the Captain commanding the party. He seemed concerned and said, 'you've got fever and must go back to Delhi'. A two-bullock cart was procured and off I bumped for a 16 mile drive across rough country with no roads for miles. On yes! - I had fever all right! It was Malaria and in a few minutes I began to feel full of aches and pains and I did not enjoy the ride in the bullock cart. That bout laid me out for ten days.

I was supposed to return to work, taking it a bit easy, but never one for sitting about, I went off on a crocodile hunt. The River Jumna has man-eaters in it, and these are snubbed-nosed. The other varieties are fish-eaters with long noses. The Colonel had a heavy flat punt and loaned it to me. Out on the river a crocodile arose a few feet away from me and as it was snubbed-nosed I took a shot at it. The crocodile submerged and rose under the punt and nearly overturned it. It then appeared alongside the punt and started to have a go at the woodwork. With my rifle almost vertical and nearly touching his head I fired and the beast sunk like a stone. Crocodiles were considered pests in those days but nowadays they do have a degree of protection. My malaria seemed to have passed and my trip on the river was just the tonic I needed.

As a Lieutenant I was made Adjutant of the Regiment, a position I held for the next six years until I was promoted to Captain. The authorities did things rather slowly. In 1861 the Regiment had been in China and twenty years later the campaign medal was issued, and a fine time I had trying to trace discharged soldiers entitled to wear it. A small number of the medals were left over as I could not find the pensioners or their relatives and so I had to return them to base. The life of an adjutant was quite stressful and one night I dreamed that I had gone bald with all the worry. I had a good head of hair, but when I awoke in the morning most of it was on my pillow and from then on it fell out very quickly until I became quite bald at an early age. The Indian sun is quite fierce and so I found if prudent to wear a hat, or suffer a sunburnt scalp.

We received orders to march to Lucknow. Nothing about that march was special until we were one day out from arrival at Lucknow. We were at Oonao and rejoicing because it was already getting hot. That night one of the Carters, a native, went down with cholera. The orders were to stay where we were for ten days after the discharge of the last case. The campsite had a well with a brick wall round it and the day after the Carter recovered we found him washing his clothes in the well. It is a miracle that the whole unit wasn't infected; we all had a lucky escape. Whilst at the campsite we had a dust storm. I had paraded the regiment and the C.O. asked me to ride his horse, as he thought it would be good for it to have some experience of parade work. It was a nice little Arab and in the middle of this parade the dust storm blew up. Within minutes it was a howling gale and I couldn't see beyond the horse's ears. The beast got quite alarmed and so I patted it on the neck to console it and was surprised to get an electric shock every time I touched the horse. I suppose the saddle insulated me but the wild weather had certainly electrified the horse   Anyway it appeared to have suffered no ill-effects. As soon as the storm had passed over I noticed our dining table outside the mess tent looked as it someone had stood alongside it with a spade and shovelled six inches of soil on top of it.

Eventually we reach Lucknow albeit somewhat late. It was quite an interesting place. The Residency, battered in the Mutiny, is the only place in the British Empire where the flag flies day and night. I wonder how much longer it will do so.

Two things happened to me at Lucknow. I got married and we experienced a tornado. Real, not marital! It happened at night so there would have been many casualties and it lasted for about ten minutes. The trees all had their leaves stripped from them by a violent shower of hail and then the winds simply blew them over. Every road was bordered by cork trees and not one of them was left standing, and they blocked the roads completely. In my garden I was nurturing several rows of potatoes and these were blown completely out of the ground. I never located one of them. Most of the bungalows were thatched and these roofs were ripped off and left lying upside down looking as if a giant had picked up the thatch with a mighty finger and thumb and simply turned it over. My neighbour had a front porch that was blown so far away, it was never seen again.

Warfare in the Sudan

Trouble had been brewing for sometime in the Sudan and in February 1885 we suddenly received orders for the regiment to go to Suakin, to form part of an Indian brigade being sent there. About two days from Aden and at sea, I suppose it must have been about 7.45am, we sited an unknown island on the starboard bow and from it came an appalling stench. It was a dead whale and the pong put us off our breakfast. This would not have been remarkable except to say that at breakfast the next day another dead whale hove in sight, complete with bad smell and once again we all gave up on the idea of breakfast. A coral reef runs along most of the west side of the Red Sea, but this does have breaks in it, and the one at Suakin is just wide enough to let a ship pass through and once inside the reef the water is shallow and quiet. The shoreline is desert scrub, and flat plain for several miles inshore, which must have been covered by sea in the past, as whereever you dig you come upon a bed of white coral and most of the local houses are built from it. Now and then there are gaps in the coral inland so that you can dig down quite a way. One of our Officers had a terrible smell in his tent, and discovered he had pitched it on the grave of a recently buried camel.

As soon as we landed we heard that the cavalry had been in a scrummage with the enemy that morning and therefore we slept on the ground that night ready for action should we be attacked. The night was quiet so the next day we took the opportunity to erect our tents. The brigade under General Hudson, with the rest of the force formed a circle around the landward side of Suakin; sentries patrolling along the front. During the day we had to send working parties to unload the ships carrying our supplies. The Arabs came at night, probing our defences and one of our sentries was speared and killed. It being almost impossible to hit a man with a rifle bullet in the dark, what we wanted was some buckshot. I got our armourer to cut up some lead into little strips an inch long and about an eighth of an inch square. I stuffed these into an empty cartridge case after removing the bullet. I tested this by firing towards the ground some thirty yards away. In the distance was the General's tent and I was horrified to hear something go whirring over in his direction. The General shot out of his tent and when I tried to explain myself, I was told what I could do with my imitation buckshot!

McNeil's Zariba, or the battle of Tofrek

In 1885, my force was opening up a new road via Suakin to the River Nile. The whole force had been out for two days previously in a different direction and had fought an action at Hasheen. My own regiment in which I was the Adjutant happened to be at one time infiltrated from the right, and I noticed that a bullet embedded itself in the sand a little way from my right foot. I thought I would dig it up and was just bending down with my hand on the ground when a second bullet came and struck the same place. I thought I had better leave them undisturbed in case bullet number three should come along. The bullets were most peculiar, being made of cast iron (I have one on the table before me as I write). The Arabs had thousands of excellent rifles taken from the Egyptian

Forces killed by them. Fortunately, for us they were not expert marksmen and relied more on primitive weapons such as spears and long knives. Shortly after the incident with the bullets striking the sand a dhooly passed, with Major Wilkinson of the 9th Bengal Lancers laying wounded in it. He had been pinned into his saddle by an Arab wielding a short spear held high in the air. With both hands he drove it through the Major's thigh and into the saddle where it stuck. Soon after I met a Captain of the same regiment, accompanied by his trumpeter who had a narrow escape. These two had killed several Arabs, but one of them got under his guard with a spear and struck home in a vulnerable place. It did not penetrate, surprising both Captain Garstin and his assailant. Before the regiment left India, Mrs Garstin had sewn bits of chain mail inside his khaki tunic and the spear point had been arrested by the mail.

All this day, during which I had been mounted, I had been in agony from a painful boil on my leg which my stirrup leather continually pressed and rubbed. The next day, orders came for us to march due south and intelligence circulated information that no fighting would occur, as there was no enemy in that direction. I thankfully seized the opportunity, on the Medical Officer's advice, to remain in camp. At 2pm, I heard heavy independent firing, followed after a time by regular volleys, one after another. Volley firing is now obsolete, but at that time it was still used. Half a mile in front of me was a long line of thick bush from which came riderless horses covered with blood, galloping wildly towards our camp, quickly followed by loose mules and unwounded men and followers. Among the latter was our interpreter with a sword cut on his arm, and another man from the 15th Sikhs who had been on guard with the transport mules; most of these animals were killed. He had put his bayonet through a native and one of his thumbs was shot off. These men agreed that the whole force was destroyed; the most optimistic saying perhaps a quarter of them had escaped. Since I could still hear disciplined and regular volleys, I was not so pessimistic. An Officer came along saying we were about to be attacked and everyone should move off to the safety of the warships moored in the harbour. I rather suspected that he had no authority to issue these orders and I decided to ignore them and my men and I remained where we were. I got them to entrench and build cover with ammunition boxes and food stores etc. Night came on and nothing happened. The next morning I was relieved and rejoiced to see the whole force return. The 15th Sikhs came in marching with fixed bayonets, many of them broken and bent and their faces blackened with gunpowder. I received them into camp with a great cheer. They were keen to tell me what had happened and presently I knew the whole story, as if I had been there myself. Subsequently, we traversed the same ground and there were piles of dead several feet high still lying about. We then went on to Tamai and we had a fight there, which we finished by burning the place down. As the firing of the huts proceeded we were attacked by rifle, wild independent firing appearing to arise from nowhere. Eventually we figured it out. The enemy had hidden their ammunition in the thatched roofs of the - by now - blazing huts. I have a cartridge with 'Tamai' scratched on it also lying on my table as I write. Some of this exploding ammunition hit our men and I can still see our surgeon with his finger up to the hilt in a man's body trying to fish one these bullets out. When the force reached Tofrek, we made three sides of a huge square, the left formed by the 17th Bengal Infantry. Next them to them and in front were the Madras Sappers, then the Berkshires and the 15th Sikhs. A battalion of the Grenadier Guards and some others formed the right side. The Hussars were scouting in front, but the bush was so thick that they could not do much or penetrate it in depth, as they would have lost touch. The Madras Sappers and Miners were sent, unarmed, to the front and began clearing the bush with billhooks (this was thorny acacia), to build a Zariba - a thorny enclosure. The Berkshires were told to pile arms and to go forward and cut wood too. The remainder of the force received orders to stack arms and fall out. Colonel G.R. Hennessy, (later General) our C.O. did not do this. He ordered the men to fix bayonets and to keep their rifles in their hands and remain seated in ranks on the ground. Presently one of the Hussars galloped in asking where the General was, as the enemy were in the bush. A second Hussar followed, shouting 'they are right behind me in swarms!' Peering at the dense bush I could see nothing, and then the Vedettes galloped out of the bush with the enemy among them, one rider with a native on the back of his horse trying to get his spear into him, but frustrated by the jolting of the horse and having to hang on to the rider. The unfortunate sappers out there, unarmed, cutting wood, were caught and slaughtered. The Berkshires met almost the same fate, but numbers of them rushed back to their piled arms and began to fight back. Out front we later discovered one of the sapper's officers, Newman by name, was found dead, lying in an aggressive attitude with gritted teeth and clenched fists, showing how he died.

The main Arab attack came diagonally on the left corner of the square. The 17th Bengal Infantry were broken and their C.O. killed, and some of the Arabs were now inside the square and behind us. The men in our rear ranks turned about and sorted them out with the bayonet. Some of our men were killed, including the C.O.'s Syce (Groom), the horse blankets he was carrying had seventeen spear holes through it. One of the Officers of the Bengals was knocked over onto his back in the Arab charge and every Arab that ran over him made a thrust or cut at his body. He parried everyone, and got up afterwards with nothing but a minor scratch. Thanks to Colonel Hennessey we were ready, and our men opened a tremendous fire with their Sinders, and if a bullet from one those hit you, you did not get up. Our men were absolutely 'up' for this battle. A Havildar dashed into the middle of the Arabs, bayoneted four of them and then resumed his place in the ranks. This gallant fellow was a most stupid man at ordinary duties and I have lost count of the times I had to tell him off, but in the future I tempered by corrections, remembering how brave he had been.

An Indian Officer, Subadar Gurdet Singh (a volunteer from the 45th Sikhs) cut down one Arab with his sword which split the man almost in half to the top of his head to his waist. He did the same with the second Arab and then a third, and then his sword broke (Lord Wolseley subsequently presented him with a new one with a suitable inscription on it). One of our men lost his head and when his body was brought in, his head was carried separately in a handkerchief. Our firing was so heavy the barrels became red hot, and a Sepoy was so badly burnt on the hand he had to be invalided back to India. We had 21 killed and wounded, a small number compared to others who had been caught with piled arms and some of them larking about.

The Arab attack being broken on the left, the survivors sheared off to our right and the last heavy firing was the volleys of the Grenadier Guards, although some odd shots went on for some time. The Arabs lost hundreds, mainly in the front of the left corner of the square and that action broke Osman Digna's power of good. His men never made any large attacks after that, though we had several smaller actions now and then.

A few months later most of the force was withdrawn from Suakin, but my lucky Regiment was selected to remain behind all through the hot weather and was it hot indeed, about 130 in the shade. The sappers built a double-roofed wooden hut over our Mess Tent, but it was still boiling hot. Our water ration was 1 gallon per man per day. This was distilled seawater and was left in an iron tank in the sun, so that when we got it, it was already warm. This ration was for washing, cooking and drinking.
Some of you Sybarites can think of that when you complain of the heat.

Our conditions were so terrible several men committed suicide. The flies added to our misery. At meal times you could not see what was on your plate, as the food would be covered with a swarming mass of black insects. To make a fly trap we placed a little of our water sweetened with sugar in a bucket and in a short time the bucket would be full of drowned flies. These would be carried away and buried in a pit until the ground heaved over the decomposing mass beneath.

We were occasionally in action but things quietened down by the end of May, and in October we were relieved by the Madras Regiment and returned to India. We used to read in the newspapers of how 'comforts for the troops' were being shipped to us, items like fruit etc. We did not receive much in the way of such comfort. My Subadar came to me with a piece of watermelon about as big as a fist, saying 'Sahib, there are 64 men in my company. How am I to divide this?' I told him to give each of them a pip and keep the rest for himself! We were sent some tea, cocoa, and tinned milk. The men liked it, although I did not partake of any as they had simply boiled the whole lot up together. I should imagine it had a strange flavour.

Nowshera

This place is noted for extremes of temperature, very cold in winter, and very hot in summer. We were taken there by train and on arrival the door of one of the carriages, the men had been in was found to have been torn off during the night and none of the men, such was the depth of their sleep, could offer an explanation. The house I was allotted was about 18 months old. It had no garden just a waste of sand and shingle with a few tuffs of 'tub' which is a good edible grass for livestock, and there was one small tamarisk bush. It looked as though nothing would ever grow there. As we were to be there for eighteen months I thought I would make an effort to improve the place. I had a Persian watermill installed and put in a few young mulberry trees. (Editor's note: A Persian watermill relies on earthenware jars, fitted to a rotating wheel, wind or animal powered, which lifts water up from a well). I employed a Mali (gardener) to put in a few seeds and the result was magical. It was virgin soil just awaiting cultivation and in six months I had the best garden in the place. I am glad that I did this planting as we were, unknown to us at the time, to stay there for four years and the little mulberry trees had grown so big that the Mali's boy was able to climb them. I told the Mali he could help himself to the vegetables as long as we had an adequate supply. During the hot weather my wife used to go to Murree in the hills taking with her the two young children who were born during our stay at Nowshera. After an absence of five months she returned to the house and complained that the little tree she had planted had disappeared, I said "no it hasn't look up", she was standing underneath it. Cabbages, cauliflowers, turnips, peas, beans, artichokes, everything grew. If you pulled a carrot it was at lease a foot long. I said to the Mali "any chance of some beetroot?" He scratched his head and said "I will do my best Sir". The next morning was a large bed of full grown beetroot. I was suspicious as to which neighbour's garden the beetroot had come from, but there were no complaints so we kept quiet. In the hot weather it was 110 in the house and we had to contend with dust storms. These were like blasts from a furnace. Elsewhere in India a shower of rain usually follows a dust storm, but not at Nowshera. I was looking through my window glass during a dust storm and as I watched I saw a line of sunflowers turn black and wilt. Despite the heat I managed to grow gallons of watercress in such abundance that I supplied the Officers' Mess. Nowshera is not very far from Attak. The river Indus runs past it and the Kabul River joins it there. My father who had been there years previously told me he had seen both rivers in flood and that millions and millions of rats were drowned and these dead bodies covered the planes for miles around, so much so that riding was dangerous as the horse tended to slip on the greasy bodies. These are the extremes of India. I have gone into the stables wearing light coloured jodhpurs and on looking down noticed that they had turned black as thousands of fleas had been waiting the arrival of a warm blooded creature like me, luckily I managed to brush them all off. Wasps were another problem. We had 64 nests on our veranda, each the size of a golf ball. I made fruitless efforts at destroying them and my bearer whom I though was a bit of a half wit was looking on with his mouth open, and presently remarked, "that he could sort them out", so I said go ahead. To my amazement he just gathered them up in his hands crushing them as he did so, he appeared to have felt nothing. I found another nest in the bathroom, which I attempted to destroy with a burning rag on the end of a long stick. These bathroom wasps were very cunning and seemed to know what I was up to because they all dived out of the nest and straight down the open front of my shirt. I had quite a lively five minutes. I was stung considerably before I managed to sort them out. There were plenty of snakes at Nowshera, mostly cobras and one or two of those were practically albino but not quite as their eyes were black and the spectacles on their hoods were black too. At the various headquarters of Indian officials in many districts model snakes were displayed, moulded from clay and correctly coloured. These were used to educate novices. I had a set and kept them as curiosities in the dining room. One morning, going to breakfast, I found one of them on the floor near my chair and suspected my wife and put it there to scare me; I was about to pick it up when it wriggled away! Quite a good model!

We had an Indian cook; an elderly fellow who did not have a very acute sense of smell. I cannot count the number of meals we did not eat because something in it was 'off'. I told him to make an omelette with five eggs as Indian fowls' eggs are very small. The omelette had a very decided flavour so I called the cook in and asked him how many bad eggs he had put into it to which he replied "only one Sahib". On another occasion I felt that the milk was getting distinctly weaker as time went on. I called the cook in again and I told him that there was no need for him to add water to the milk, as we were quite capable of doing it ourselves. He thanked us and agreed. The milk improved wonderfully well.

Crows, again!

As you know by now I hate the beasts (crows, that is!). They just loved to torture and annoy other animals. If I sit under a tree reading a book, a crow will pick up some object and alight in the tree over my head and drop it. I had a small goat tied to one of the mulberry trees in the garden. A crow decided to play, 'here we go round the mulberry bush', but it hopped around in front of it and naturally the goat followed until it had really wound it up, at that stage being quite helpless jumped on it's head and started pecking it's nose and would have no doubt gone for its eyes had I not rescued it.

Swarms of termites hatched after a shower of rain, and the local frogs had a great feast. Two crows spotted a rather large frog and began to annoy it, one grabbed one leg and dragged it one way and the other grabbed the other let and dragged it another way, no doubt they would have killed it had I not intervened yet again. The rain had drowned some rats and one of the local kites, called a Pharaoh's chicken was beginning to dissect it. Three crows spotted this and a real play began. First of all, they did all they could to distract the kite's attention, who, being wise, paid not the slightest attention to them, but went on steadily at the rat. One crow would say look here and turning up a stone would peer beneath as if interested in a find. No response from the kite, no. 1 crow got fed up and flew off, no. 2 crow eventually gave up in disgust, and third crow popped behind the kite, grabbed hold of a beak full of tail feathers and gave three good tugs and flew off. Eventually I was rewarded by seeing a crow really getting it's comeuppance. There is in India a large bird called Adjutant Stork and it is a carrion eater. I say a stork busy with some offal accompanied by the usual crow trying to intervene, it was annoying the stork and getting ever closer to it and suddenly the stork swallowed the crow as if it had been a grain of corn. The crow, however, evidently objected to it's new surroundings and must have flapped about a bit as the stork suddenly vomited the crow back up, where it lay on the ground in a dishevelled condition until it picked itself up, re-arranged it's feathers and flew off in a huff. Needless to say I shall return to the subject of crows at a later time.

We used to have earthquakes at Nowshera, about one a month and these were fairly minor but one always got oneself outside, as you never knew quite what might happen next. My two small children were playing in the garden being shepherded by my Sikh orderly, who was very fond of them, when an earthquake suddenly started. Both children fell over and the orderly performed all sorts of antics trying to remain upright. I stood on the veranda holding on to a post and saw the whole garden moving in sort waves. Afterwards, I could find no trace in the sandy soil of a crack or fissure, there was a peculiar sulphurous smell, however, which hung in the air.

Another thing we used to have to contend with were thieves and ruffians. We were quite close to the northwest frontier and on one occasion when I was away my Sikh orderly who was sleeping on the premises was murdered by a gang of five of them. At night they attacked him and he knocked four of them down, seizing the fifth as to arrest him the man cried out for his friends to come back which they did and they shot my poor fellow twice through the back and killed him and made good their escape. The house servants from behind their barricaded doors had peered through the chinks in the woodwork and were able to tell me what happened.

Ferozepore, and more crows

We received orders to march to Ferozepore. On the way we stayed for sometime at Rawalpindi for a camp of exercise and manoeuvres. During which there was a parade with an inspecting general. A dust storm blew up and no-one could see where they were on the parade ground. Unfortunately, the horse artillery galloped past the General, or thought they did, actually they charged right over the spot that he and his staff were standing on. The General and his staff all showed an amazing turn of speed and managed to escape. My marching about was severely hampered as I had been on horseback when my mount suddenly ran into a tree, injuring my knee. It swelled up and the surgeon ordered me into a stretcher and I completed the march to Ferozepore in a dhooly, 'a stretcher'. After a few days I was still a cripple as my let would not bend so I was obliged to force it further and further until there was a loud crack and the joint returned to full movement. Ferozepore is a dusty place and the Indians have a saying, 'Peshawar Ka Sarda, Ferozepore Ka Garda' which means Pershawar for cold, Ferozepore for dust. Our poor drum major found it out when marching in front of the band leading the regiment along the road. The dust was so thick that we didn't see a bullock cart going along in the same direction. There was a stick jutting out of the back of the cart and he marched straight into it and damaged his eye. In the heat I put a thermometer onto the floor of my veranda and it went up to 161, I could have fried an egg on the floor. In the cold weather the thermometer would register 17 below freezing in the early morning. Although the land around was a flat dry plane when the monsoon broke the ground would be covered with tiny frogs. Where on earth they came from I do not know. The locals said they fell with the rain.

I was riding along on my duties when the crows turned up looking for some mischief and seeing a kite, decided to mob it. None of them actually touched the kite and the kite never touched them, despite this one of the little black beasts fell down dead. I picked it up and examined it carefully, there was not a mark on it. I believe the little monster got so excited during his gang warfare that he had a heart attack and died.

I was doing quite well in my garden as I have said. I had a pot with some prize Fresias. I was very proud of them, as very few had managed to grow them in the locality, I tended them carefully and put a label in a cleft stick in the pot, I returned to the house and to my amazement a crow flew down' pulled up the cleft stick, took my label out and ripped it in half, and then proceeded to chop up all the Fresia shoots I just managed to run out in time and scare it off. I had heard that if you catch a crow and tie it to a stick others will come down to investigate and the tethered crow would grab its would-be rescuer and then you could catch that and tether that one down until such times as you had caught the crow in the vicinity, ho ho!

One of my servants caught a crow stealing in our pantry, so we staked him out and eventually all the crows in the area turned up until my trees were black with them. They all swooped down and round the captive but never close enough for the trapped bird to grab hold of one of them. After about an hour of this and getting fed up with the noise I had to go out and release the tethered crow. It gave me a filthy look and flew off.

Kashmir

I got leave to Kashmir and on my first night I pitched my tent in a grass field, which contained a lot of white Mulberry trees. It rained in the night and we were washed out, however when the sun came out we dried out and packed up. We had several ponies with us and they liked to gorge themselves on the mulberries, which were very sweet. I gathered a pile of them and one little mare ate the lot until the juice was spilling out of her mouth on each side, strange to say, after that day she never touched another one. You would have heard about the beautiful houseboats in Kashmir. We drew the short straw. I booked one for a few days on the River Jhelum, below the town of Srinagar this seemed to be the natural sewer of the place, dead dogs, dead cats, and all manner of filth came floating by. If the level of the river falls a few inches it leaves a margin of foul dirt along the banks and it stank. In those days there was no sanitation of any kind and the condition of the streets was indescribable. Canon Tyndale-Biscoe has done marvels with his mission school there and he has turned out a number of fine characters. We moved our camp to a place called Uchabul and put the tents under some lovely plane trees. As evening descended so did the mosquitoes, but we resolved that problem by lighting smoky fires which kept them away. An Indian doctor pitched his tent near us and I invited him over for a drink. He had had quite a romantic life. During the Afghan war of 1878-81 he had been captured. The Amir made him Court Surgeon and provided him with an Afghan wife. However, he dreamt of escape and after a year managed to get away travelling by unfrequented hills and passes. En route his fame spread and the tribes people flocked to him for treatment. As he had no medicines most of his methods were pretty rough and he described to me how he operated on some of his patients, I will refrain from details! The local crafts were excellent and I bought small copper bowls, the only tools I could see these craftsmen had were a small chisel, an old nail, and a little hammer. If I had any spare cash I would have bought more of them. That night one of the copper-ware men came to my tent. At that time I was wearing a pair of velvet riding breeches, which were quite grey. He seemed quite taken with these and offered me copper pots for them. I agreed and had them washed and gave them to him the next day, as soon as he saw them his face fell as they had washed up quite white. He said he had liked the grey colour, I said don't worry just wear them for a week and they will be quite grey again, he left me some pots and went off quite happily with my old breeches.

I decided I would like a suit of the local cloth. A tailor measured me up and promised me he would have the suit ready in two days which was just as well as we were leaving. Come the morning of our departure, no tailor, no suit. We set off along a lonely road and hadn't gone far when I heard faint shouts behind me and there was the tailor in the distance running towards me with my suit. As it was a quiet road I changed into the new clothes and our cavalcade resumed its march. We passed over the Peer Punjal Pass at 11,000 feet. The most numerous wild flowers were just like bright blue dandelions but none of them had gone to seed which was a pity as I should love to have collected some.

England

I had been eleven years in India and was due to leave for England, this was 1890 and I was worried about what I should do during a whole year's leave, I hate to be idle for too long. Like other junior officers in India, where the cost of living was cheap, I used to keep several polo ponies, and now and then one of them would go sick so I thought, what about a Veterinary course. I went to the college and asked if I might attend. I also wrote to my C.O. pointing out that I had had no leave for eleven years and that if I got this course I would need six months extension to my leave. This was approved. The course was three years in those days, but by mugging up hard and attending all the lectures, three each morning, and in the afternoons we had practical work in the stables. So much of the work was similar to human medicine I began to plan taking up doctoring on my eventual retirement from the Army. I found the course most interesting and crammed three years work into one. I rejoined my regiment feeling somewhat tired but we never required the assistance of Veterinary Surgeon again. The Government thought an Indian Regiment would be suitable for duty in Hong Kong, and a regiment was raised and sent there, composed of Punjabi Moslems. My brother was appointed to it. (Ernest Cave Rowcroft, D.S.O. Late, Major 36th Sikhs). I can't remember what year that was, but he told me they marched into Hong Kong with the band playing and colours flying. The band was terrible, emitting some hideous noises. My brother complained to the band Sergeant and he replied quite airily we have some new men Sir and they are only making noises. He couldn't see anything wrong in it and said it was standard practice. My brother put him right. (Editor's note: Ernest Rowcroft took part in the march to Peking to relieve the Legations who were under attack during the Boxer revolt. 1900).

Peshawar

From Ferozpore we were sent to Peshawar. In the hot weather it was the only plains station where it was cool in the early morning. Musketry practice commenced at 5.00am and a cool breeze would blow on us from the Khyber-pass.

We occupied what was known as the last house in India from it's position at the extreme end of the mall, it leaked like hell in the rain and I remember sitting at dinner with an umbrella up. The garden was overrun with snakes and one evening as I left the bathroom I realized that I did not hear the bathroom door catch as it closed behind me. I turned to see the tail of a lizard trapped in the door, so I opened the door to release it. Bejabers! It was no lizard but a five-foot cobra. I got my stick and finished it off.

My little fox terrier, Tip, was a lovely little fellow but he had his vices. Any pith helmet he got hold of was doomed. He destroyed all the children's hats, but one day I caught him red-handed, I grabbed him and put the rim of the helmet round his neck and I gave him a scolding every hour showing him the rim and I told him he was an evil little devil and he wasn't to destroy hats again. I tied him up and he looked the picture of misery, contrition and penitence that I gave him a final warning and let him off. He jumped about with joy, went in to the next room, found my hat and ate it. The rest of the time he spent chasing squirrels and could actually climb trees by sticking his claws into the bark and hauling himself up, that is until he fell out of the tree and dislocated a paw. Well! I am a vet, aren't I! So I put his paw into a splint and on releasing him from the bandaging he promptly climbed the same tree on three legs. That's dogs for you!

As far as the regiment was concerned, things were pretty quiet except one of the men, a Moslem bandsman cut his wife's throat one night, and not content with that, did his mother-in-law and his wife's sister in the same way. This was a quite deliberate action as he actually went to the trouble of holding a basin underneath them to catch the blood. I never liked him much; I thought he looked a bit shifty and I am sorry to say my suspicions were confirmed. After a trial he was duly hanged.

Chitral Relief Expedition

The 14th Sikhs (Ferozpore) were beleaguered in the fort at Chitral in 1895. We left Hoti Mardan near Peshawar and our route was via Mulakund Pass, beyond which English footsteps had never trod, consequently the maps supplied were a little sketchy. Our Commanding Officer was General Low, C.B. The Mulcand Pass had first to be stormed. This was done in the usual way, the ridges on each side running down into Indian Territory being first crowned by our troops who fought their way up. The tops stood at 4,000 feet and the enemy tribesmen held the top of the Pass building stone breastworks from which to fire at us. Our cavalry made a feint some distance off and I had a stiff climb whilst the enemies attention was diverted. There was no one there, the enemy had slipped away, but judging by the amount of blood on the rocks he must have been carrying many dead and wounded. We followed them down and into the Swat Valley. The next day the guides' cavalry got into some of them and thinned them out. In the meantime, a track unknown to us was discovered leading over the Pass and for the next day or two working parties toiled from morn until night getting our supplies up. I discovered an Indian Guard of a few men with a couple of mules and some chests sat around on the track. I asked them what they were doing and was told they were escorting the pay chest of the Sappers and Miners. One of their mules was dead and they were gasping for water. I pointed out a spring among the rocks and I recall filling my water bottle several times and consuming it. Since my water bottle held a quart I think I must have drunk just under a gallon. I got an empty bucket and watered the surviving mules, didn't they just drink. I had to repeat this several times and then I gave them a bale of hay. After this, we got the treasure chest onto their backs and they went up the track. I saw several mules fall off the precipice, poor brutes. They were chained in sets of three and as one fell over it took the other two with it. I remained on that track all day assisting baggage parties until it became quite dark, and I realised I was all alone on a hostile hillside so I began to very quietly and very carefully make my way up and over the Pass to our encampment. Tribesmen could have been prowling about; luckily I did not run into them. Later on we found an excellent road, much of it hewn from solid rock, this was said to hve been made by Alexander the Great. We had camels as baggage animals as well as the mules, these were linked in sets of five. One day our Transport Officer told one of the camel drivers off for not looking after his animals better. Sahib, he said, "what do I know about camels, I am a baker", that was the insane way out transport used to be organised when an expedition suddenly cropped up. The next day part of the force started off to cross the Swat River and take the village of Chukdara on the opposite side and some eight miles higher up the Valley. The Valley was cultivated with rice which was at that time shooting green and a few inches high. My regiment was left in camp in reserve. I had just started my breakfast and I could hear the guns when a young staff officer came galloping back shouting for us to come on, he would lead the way. We fell in columns of companies and marched off. After two or three miles the Staff Officer left us saying, "head towards the sound of the guns", and he rode off. We marched straight into a swamp, some of the men went in up to their waists. The men on firmer ground undid their puttees and using them as ropes pulled their comrades to safety. I got a bit bogged down but managed to get myself out. Onwards we went and at the next stream I managed to fall in accidentally, head first, and I got rid of all the mud from the swamp. The weather was so hot I soon dried out.

At last we reached the force in front and halted half a mile below Chukdara. Low hills running close by were crowded by the enemy who kept up a continuous fire on us. In those days officers had to set a good example to their men. It was not considered proper for an Officer to take cover, so I had to saunter about with an air of nonchalance. I got my men under cover, whilst I had to parade about in the open. I was wincing inside expecting any minute to be shot, but merciful providence protected me then as on numerous other occasions. Since the ground was soft bullets striking the earth went in without raising dust and the enemy could not see where their shot fell, so fire slackened off. We did not fire back as they were too well covered and it would have been a waste of ammunition. Suddenly, a burst of terrific firing began; I turned round to see that the 11th Bengal Lancers had suddenly appeared behind us. This was too good a target for the enemy to miss and the cavalry took some casualties before wisely deciding to clear off.

I suddenly heard the terrific beating of drums and I looked up the valley to see thousands of tribesmen, marching in fours, with drums and flags coming towards us. On and on they came and it looked as if our bayonets would be used in earnest.

All this time the Sappers were busy preparing a floating bridge for the force to cross by, as the river was deep. Presently, Brigadier General Waterfield rode up and ordered our C.O. to take five men and try to find a ford in the river. Some fifteen minutes later, the Brigadier came back and said to me, "Rowcroft take the regiment and cross the river", I said "yes Sir, and what am I to do when I get across?" He said, "Take the village!" So I replied "very good Sir" and off we went expecting to run into the mob of tribesmen I had seen a few minutes before. I couldn't see a ford, but concluded it must be opposite the village. I ordered the men to link arms and go over. I and our Indian Adgutant, a fine young Sikh, grasped each others arms and waded in. The water came up to our chests and it was running pretty swiftly. The bottom consisted of slippery boulders and how we kept our feet I do not know. At this point the river was about 100 yards wide. Can just see our Medical Officer a tall, shake the water out of his watch, so I knew the water was deep (a couple of days later the M.O.'s watch stopped and the Armourer fixed his eye glass to his right eye opened the watch and peered into it. Taking some tweezers he picked out a flea and snapped the watch shut, after which the watch kept perfect time). On gaining the other side, I turned round to see an appalling site as some of our men lost their footing and were washed away. Fortunately, there was a bend in the river a hundred yards further down, and the men were washed onto this point, all of them still clutching their rifles. I think the river was in spate as the next day troops crossed without problems. We formed up, marched off, and all in all crossed another four rivers but none of them were so dangerous as that first one. The Fourth Sikhs Regiment crossed the river higher up and had one or two men shot and one drowned. The Eleventh Bengal Lancers plunged in and crossed below us. I then found myself at the foot of a series of rising and cultivated terraces on top of which was the village of Chukdara. I sent a company around each flank and with the rest of the men went straight on up the terraces. I tried to take a short cut and immediately sank into a rice paddy up to my thighs. I had to be pulled out. Not a shot was fired at us and seeing a long low wall ahead of me I thought the opposition was gathered behind it. I ordered bayonets to be fixed and advanced in line to the wall, there was no one there. When we got to the village all doors and windows were closed, I shoulder charged a door which collapsed and I fell in head first, sword in one hand and revolver in the other. Expecting to be stabbed in the back, so I regained my feet very quickly. My brave Sikh soldiers came rushing in behind me shouting "kill them, kill them" I hastily ordered no unarmed folk were to be hurt. Several unarmed men came forward and salaamed, whilst several terror stricken women tried to hide behind cupboards and furniture. I admired the pluck of the men and pitied the poor women. No one to fight here then. On and on we went breaking into houses but finding only non-combatants.

At last we came to a large padlocked door leading into a big courtyard, a man came and begged us to leave it alone, I ignored him and broke the door open, I looked in, oh what a surprise, it was full of the village women, all sat down awaiting their fate! We left them alone and left at the far end of the village. In the distance I could see the enemy massed on the hills in the distance. Itwould seem that the marching men I had previously seen had been spooked by our cavalry and decided to make for the higher ground and safety. I received an order to take two companies and follow the cavalry. I wasn't too happy as it had been a long day and I had a whopping great blister on my foot where my ammunition boot had rubbed it sore. When I was able to take my boots off the next day, I also found that I was minus a big toe nail, that had been torn off whilst I was crossing the river, orders being orders, I marched off again and entered a splendid field of tall standing wheat. Our cavalry had gone through this previously and it was full of dead bodies. At one place I found a chieftain surrounded by his dead warriors, all of them lanced. He had a handsome ivory mounted dagger, which I removed. At that, a sharp fire was opened on us from the hills on our right by a company of a British Regiment. They must have been blind and I can hear the bullets now as they hissed through the wet corn, but none of us were shot.

Eventually after going about a mile and a half we reached a hamlet on a mound and entrenched. Presently some Sowars (Cavalry men) appeared, carrying a badly injured comrade. He had been pursuing two of the enemy and lanced one of them, when the other man fell down a long blind well. He and his horse also went down it and he was the only survivor. We sent him back on a stretcher. Then a girl of about twelve appeared. She had been speared in the back, but it was a minor wound. I can only imagine that running along with her cloak streaming out behind her, her pursuer hadn't been able to tell if she was a girl. We subsequently escorted her back to safety, and after that, looking to ourselves, we procured four sheep in this hamlet and took them back for dinner, or we would have done, had not our cavalry reappeared and they took two of our sheep. We camped for the night round Chukdara and a foraging party produced lentils, rice, onions and potatoes. We took part of one of the sheep and gave the rest to the men. One of the drummers cooked everything in a huge pot and it was dark before we ate. We had nothing since our breakfast, but even so that leg of mutton was as tough as old boots. It was too much for my constitution but one of our subalterns, a regular wolf, hacked chunks off it with a pocket knife. He was still alive the next morning (as a Major he was killed in France. He became so crippled by rheumatism he couldn't walk. He was carried into the trenches where he was wounded. The men insisted on carrying him back, although he implored them to look after themselves, which they wouldn't, and presently he received another bullet which killed him). The remains of the stew was saved for breakfast, but when our C.O. saw it in the light of day he took one look and threw up.

From Chukdara we were sent on to Punjkora where we remained in camp with some other units guarding the route over the river. We used to be attacked at night. Some of the tribesmen got amongst our camp followers and a transport driver was slashed from head to foot so badly he had to hold his stomach back in until the cut was stitched. He fully recovered from hiswounds and I came across him years later in India. While in camp here I was bowled over by a sharp attack of malaria. Our tents reached 118 in temperature and my temperature was 108, so I didn't notice the heat much. Shortly after we marched back with the rest of the force to India. I went down with another bout of malaria, the worst I've ever had, and I was put into the field hospital near Chukdara. I soon found that I couldn't lie on my left side without starting a severe pain in the right. This continued for some days and nights until at last I got desperate. I shifted around on my bed and suddenly there was a sort of crack, the sound of something giving way, and the pain completely stopped. My liver had contracted an adhesion which my movements had finally caused to give way. I was sent back to India in a stretcher and put in base hospital at Cherat, in the low hills at about 3000 feet, near Nowshera. Here I remained with Typhoid fever and after that I went down with dysentery. Eventually the powers that be sent me on a years sick leave to England. On my return I was sent Amritsar to command a detachment of two companies. Here I found myself acting as a third class Cantonment Magistrate. The proceedings were delightfully simple. The villain would be marched in by a sort of Indian Beadle, and the case began. I had before me a small book in which the briefest details were added, name, offence, plea, witnesses, etc. The guilty man would say, after sentence had been passed "the Sahib has heard me and done his best, but I have been unlucky it is my kismet". I think today a mountain of paperwork would be required and everything recorded in triplicate and all for the same result. After my court duty I was walking in the countryside when I met an Indian goatherd and we sat down together and had a chat. He had been on the Chitral Relief Expedition and had been wounded and received no compensation. He opened his coat and showed me numerous scars. I then recognized him as the transport driver who had been cut up in the night attack on our camp. He said one man had held him down whilst another repeatedly stabbed him. His survival is a miracle.

I wrote a stinging letter to the pay department and was very pleased when the goatherd came to me and said "thank you Sahib, I have received payment for my injuries". With my duty here complete I was sent back to Ferozepore by train. The Indians have an annoying habit of getting in and out of trains by the windows. We had pulled into a station and I was trying to sleep, a foot came in the window and nearly trod on my face. I gently pushed it back and explained to the owner in my best Punjabi that he really ought to be a good fellow and use the door.

Dalhousie

I got a couple of months leave to Dalhousie. The hills here are covered with red flowered rhododendrons, from which I was told an excellent jelly could be made. You have to be careful to get the right kind as some of the other plants are poisonous and will send you mad. I decided not to touch any of it, so you cannot attribute any of my subsequent lunacy to that source. My convalescence here could not be attributed to our cook because he bought 200 second hand eggs cheap at an auction. He had buried them in a heap of ashes and produced one or two as required. After a series of rotten egg omelettes I suggested what he could do with the rest of the eggs.

Near Dalhousie is a small lake, which the locals told us, was bottomless. We got a boat out and using a large fishing reel and a weight measured the depth, nowhere was it deeper than 14 feet. So much for folkfore!

I went over to the native state of Chumba to do some fishing in the river Ravi. I went to a collection of huts at a place called Burmaor at about 14,000 feet. The track leading to it was very steep and one of my ponies, a little grey mare fell over and was killed. At Burmaor the hills were rugged and steep and the river Ravi was quite unfishable as the water tore down the valley like a millrace. It was all foam. We camped here for a while, but I heard that in winter the locals all clear off for better weather elsewhere. It seems they pen their cattle in huts with numerous bales of hay and there they remained bottled up. The bears then come down and the doors of the huts are marked by numerous claw marks as the bears try to get at the cattle within. I climbed up through the pinewoods above us until I came out on the summit which was a long sharp knife edge. It was at this point that I caught sight of my first mecanopsis, a beautiful blue poppy. Years later I saw two or three specimens in a rock garden atKew, but these were not as good as the vigorous plants I saw in the wild. Speaking of poppies, some of our men used to take a little opium, very moderately. My Havildar (Sargeant) had a large thumb nail under which he kept a globule of opium and it was indeed odd to see him walking about sucking his thumb. My Bugler was a serious addict and when we were posted off on active service, he was told he couldn't come. He begged and pleaded and then fell on the ground and said I will die and burst into floods of tears. He was allowed to go and never touched opium during the whole of the campaign.

The Tirah

This minor war of 1897-98 was one of the biggest trans-frontier campaigns to occur in Victorian times but I suppose today few people would have heard of it. I shall not record the whole event, merely what happened to me. One evening I received an order to take one of our Companies and some mules to form a foraging party. Similar detachments from other regiments were also to join in, Senior Officer present to command the whole. On parade I found I was the senior. My orders were to go in a certain direction and collect what grain we could get. We had to cross a number of spurs running down from the hills boarding one side of the Tirah Valley. There were numerous villages dotted about and the nearer ones had been checked by other parties on previous days, so I had to go a long way before commencing operations. My plan was simple, as we came to each village I told off a party to load up with grain and to return to camp protecting themselves as necessary. My party, the Fifteenth Sikhs, would take the furthest village. When we reached it a Staff Officer said that it had been cleared out a day or two before, so we went on and on, a very long way. By this time I put out a small advanced piquet of a Havildar and four men, 200 yards in front, and flankers on my left and right. All of a sudden a bullet whistled through the air and struck a rock near the Staff Officer. He put spurs to his horse and we never saw him again. We then took up a defensive position. In our hurry to get under cover I did not realise we were walking on the roofs of some low houses. The mules began to sink through the thatch and the enemy opened up a furious fire on us. I took a rifle and kneeling in a line in the middle of my men began to return fire, a message was shouted back to say that one of the picket in front was wounded and at that moment a bullet took off the fingers of the man on my right. A second message was shouted out, another man in the piquet in front was wounded. The loaded mules were now behind us so I ordered everyone to retire. Carrying our wounded we were in a pretty sorry condition. We had to cross a small nullah (ravine) and then get up on to a flat bit of ground about a 150 yards square beyond which we should have more low ground to pass. It was on this flat bit the Indian Jemadar of the company was hit, I asked him if he could keep up and he said yes, but a few yards further on I saw him stagger and fall as he was shot again. I noticed one of our wounded was missing and asked the men where he was. He had been left in the nullah as they were too exhausted to carry him any further under fire. I bade the party stat where they were and made them lie down as there was no cover, and went back to look for the wounded man. I offered a prayer, as I did not expect to return alive. I reached the nullah and found the sepoy laying in a rut. He had been hit several times and was unconscious and died in my arms. I returned to my men. We still had an unladen mule so I put the wounded Jemadar on it with the assistance of a sepoy. The sepoy was shot and fell, and the Jemadar collapsed on the ground. I called a second man to come and help me. At this moment a shot struck the ground just under the mule's nose, throwing a shower of dust into it's face so it bolted carrying the Jemadar with the second sepoy hanging onto it's head. He managed to get it back to me but then he too was shot down. All in all I lost three men wounded before I could get the Jemadar to safety. The man I sent back with the mule was to ask the C.O. to send two Companies to reinforce me, as I had very few unwounded men by this time. Shots were striking quite close to me, but I was mercifully preserved. With a rifle I joined in the defence of our little party. On my right was a wounded Sikh with his leg absolutely shattered, who nevertheless continued firing until he died. On my left was one of the remaining unwounded men keeping up a furious fire. Bullets continually struck the ground a few inches in front of our head, and the Sikh would close his eyes and bob his head to avoid the shower of grit. Each time I thought 'now he's killed!', but he bobbed up every time smiling, and continued firing. How the shots ricocheted over our heads. The enemy had our range to a yard and took cover most skilfully and although I used my field glasses I rarely saw anyone, so could only direct the men to fire where I thought they must be. The shimmering heat haze also made visibility poor. We were under fire from two sides and I thought a bayonet charge might shift them, but realised we were too exhausted for that. It was afternoon now and we had no food since dawn and we had been marching, working and fighting in the hot sun for hours. If we could have shifted 70 yards to the rear we would have been undercover, my wounded men begged me not to leave them (I will not go into what the tribesmen did to our wounded men with knives, nor will I relate what their women do, which is worse) so, of course, the thought of leaving them never entered my head. I had, however, quite given up hope of ever getting back to camp, and thought it was only a question of time before we were all wiped out. I think we must have hit some of the enemy, but they still came on, I could see them creeping towards us through the long grass. At last, at about 3.30pm two companies arrived from camp, commanded by Captain Gordon. He halted them under cover of the plateau edge, and came along alone to see me, I told him to get down as the enemy had our range, and to prove it, as I passed him a rifle, a bullet struck it. Gordon concluded that we wanted the whole regiment, and sent back orders. In the meantime, we began to drag the wounded back under cover. Gordon and I picked up one and I tripped over a clod of earth. Gordon said have you been shot, and I said no. On we went with our burden and soon got under cover. Another rescue party started off with a second wounded man, but had only gone a few yards when one of them was shot down. On and on we went with this procedure and gradually we cleared the plateau of our wounded. The rest of the regiment arrived and the C.O. seeing me covered with the blood of the wounded asked if I had been shot. When I got into camp I undressed, emptied the blood out of my boots and had a good wash (one year later I was putting on my sword belt, and I discovered a large clot of dried blood on the inside of it. I had to have a word with my servant as he must have cleaned the belt fifty times and hadn't noticed the blood clot). Once we got clear of the plateau the enemy did not molest us any more. In camp I did a role call and was horrified to find a man missing. He had been on the left flank, we recovered his body the next day and I regret to say it was mutilated. We had done our job and had secured an immense amount of grain. None of the other foraging parties had had a single shot fired at them, my company bore the whole brunt, but the enemy never got past us. And so to bed, the enemy keeping up their nightly serenade of stray rifle shots throughout the night.

Our force consisted of thirty thousand troops and we were all camped in the main Tirah Valley. Expeditions would be sent out to outlaying districts, the troops returning the same day, or a day or two later. The main camp was surrounded by piquets and outposts in the middle of the valley. Every night the enemy kept up a continued fire on the camp from the hills and we had a number of casualties in this way.

The fighting was of the usual trans frontier kind. We attacked the enemy. He ran away. We retreated; he would come after us, harassing the rear guard every step of the way, and making the removal of the wounded difficult. Death by slow torture would be the fate of any one left behind, though I did hear of one case, a British Sergeant, accidentally left behind, who was well treated, and became quite friendly with his rough captors. A large force went to the head of the valley with the usual flankers on either side, and on they went into the Waran Valley beyond. I camped here, but our regimental transport nearly got lost as the road was hopeless, mostly a narrow rock strewn ravine that even the mules found difficult. Consequently, it was dark before they arrived with the rear guard, and not knowing where we were passed us by and penetrated nearly a mile further into enemy country. Suspecting that they were lost I put out a Bugler who sounded every few minutes and hearing the call our lost men found our camp.

The next morning, we were busy burning and blowing up village chieftains' houses. On our retreat the 3rd Gurkhas became our rear guard and a stiff time of it they had, the enemy pressing them every foot of the way. As we approached the demarcation line the valley on the Waran side got very narrow until it was about a hundred yards across on either side of this were bare cloud terraces with no cover from above. I received an order to take a company and occupy one or two huts and to remain there to let the rear guard pass. My company was a depleted one and I got them all into a building with a sort of roofed verandah bounded by a two feet six wall on the sides facing the enemy and on the left. The latter looked straight down into another valley, with houses dotted about. I had my men kneeling behind the verandah wall, but the enemy occupied the other houses and kept up a furious fire on us. I don't think they could see my men, but I was standing up behind them, as usual doing the British Officer thing. All this time the main body of our retiring force kept trooping past the terraces below on our right side and shielded from the enemy. In front of us was a good deal of rocky ground at about one hundred yards and it was there that I reckoned we would come head to head with the enemy. I broke a hole in the wall at the back of us ready for our escape and I sent off some of our men including the Subadar who had a damaged artery in his chest from which he subsequently died. At this stage I had a dozen men left with me. The main body had all passed, infantry, Sappers, mountain artillery, and the Gurkha rear guard and behind them the enemy and we opened fire. That stopped them and we were pretty busy for some time. I kept my eye on the Gurkhas, at length I saw the last of them disappear over the ridge. They were absolutely cooked and just collapsed on the ground until they got their breath back. I told my chaps to start a heavy fire until I gave a signal to stop, when they were to sneak back, crouching low so as not to be seen, and then out through the hole I had made in the wall, and away to safety. This we succeeded in doing. The enemy never spotted this and remained where they were thinking we were laying an ambush to them. Not so! We were running over heavy ploughed land for over half a mile and were somewhat tired by being heavily armed and accoutred. I kept wondering when the shots were going to come at us from the rear and as we were all bunched together on the narrow terrace they couldn't have missed us, however, we all got away without a man being hit.

My regiment then took over as rear guard. It was now late in the afternoon and the enemy then came after us in swarms, we halted and faced them. The artillery took up a position behind us and their shells soon came whistling over our heads towards the enemy. In due time our C.O. Colonel Abbott gave the order to retire. At this the Senior Indian Officer, the Subadarh-Major shouted, "No! nows our chance!", and it was! There is no love lost between Sikhs and Afridies! But we couldn't stay there all evening. The C.O. then received a charge of slugs and chopped up telegraph wire full in the face followed by a bullet in the neck. His orderly wept at the sight of his wounded master and one or two other men tried to get him into a stretcher, this he refused but had to be escorted back to camp. Some of the men went berserk and I saw two of them dragging our wounded away by the legs, the wounded man's head bumping from rock to rock.

Our line of retreat lay over a succession of terraces, some of which had walls six to eight feet high and progress over this broken ground was difficult, not to say dangerous. Our Medical Officer hurt one of his legs severely falling off one of these walls. We approached the large village and I decided the best thing we could do was to take it and spend the night there. Our second in command had been out of action for some weeks, and as the C.O. was now wounded I was in command. As the enemy was shooting at us from the huts and I did not want our troops to go firing in the dark, I ordered bayonets to be fixed. I gave the order "prepare to charge"! the men let out a loud cheer. As I ran forward in the dark I found myself trampling on bodies and presently I fell over one. My elbow hit the ground and set off my revolver which was in my left hand, my sword being in my right. One of my men dashed over me and he halted just long enough to see if I was not an enemy to be bayoneted. Up I leapt and on into the village. The enemy retreated but continued firing from cover, we dashed into the huts and Captain Lewarne, who was along side me called out "Oh!" and fell dead, he had been shot through the heart. To our surprise we found a small party of the Thirty sixth Sikhs had joined us in our charge, their C.O. Colonel Haughton, being with them. He and his Adjutant were killed a few days later. One of their Subalterns, Munn, was also with the party, he ran his sword into a tribesman but it was wrenched out of his hand and he lost it. Moral, always secure your sword knot firmly round your wrist. The next minute a bullet tore off his little finger.

At the same time, unknown to us, a party of Dorsets were occupying the other end of the village. Presently they left it and one by one, scrambled into a ravine. An educated voice called to the Dorsets to come along. Actually, it was a party of tribesmen waiting for them at the end of the ravine, one of them an English speaker. One by one the Dorset men were cut down. All except Private Vickery who made such a fight of it that he escaped with a portion of an Afridi's skull on the end of his bayonet. Private Vickery received his Victoria Cross from Queen Victoria herself. A strange thing happened to one of the Thirty sixth Sikhs. I have heard this happening rarely. One of the enemy's bullets entered the muzzle of his rifle. Beyond a bit of a jar, he was quite uninjured, though I suppose his rifle became useless. I distributed my men as best I could in the dark and lay down. The continued cries of the wounded, it was impossible to attend to them in the dark and the cold weather, we were dressed in cotton khaki and it was 17 below, made sleep impossible. The next day we went out to get the wounded. One of these was our Senior Havildar Signaller, an excellent fellow who was very brave in action. He was shot through both thighs and told me he had been calling out all night, but none of us heard him.

As soon as it was light enough, Colonel Haughton, of the 36th who was now Senior Officer present, instead of sending out a small reconoitering patrol to investigate the ground ahead. He started out alone, so I feld bound to accompany him. We had hardly gone beyond the village when a shot was fired by an Afridi from a few yards range to our right. Colonel Haughton, was very deaf, and did not hear the shots. The bullet whizzed by my knees and struck a rock on my left. He must have been just a sentry as there was no one else about and no further shots were fired at us. We got all the wounded together and began to retire and the enemy at once started following on, and firing on us. A force came out from camp and relieved us. I think we had 30 casualties, mostly our Indian Officers, and we only had a few left. Because of this our regiment was sent back alone to Ferozepore.

Ferozepore and Red Tape

Back at base, I found myself commanding my regiment. The Commanding Officer had several slugs still imbedded in his face and he retired. The second in command was wounded and sent to England so that is how I ended up leading the regiment. Everyday I expected to hear of someone being put over me, but I was left undisturbed in high office!

Junior Officers joined us from England and I welcomed them to the Mess, one young man, I noticed, would never eat toast. I asked him about it one breakfast and he explained that after landing in India he happened to pass an open kitchen door and saw a man making toast by a fire, using his toes as the toast rack. The second in command was granted another year's leave and on top of that a third. I had a year's leave in England and when I came back I found myself still the Commanding Officer at which time he retired. So there I was, commanding an Infantry Regiment as a Captain. I was made temporary Major and eighteen months' later I was confirmed in that rank with 20 years' service. Three years' later, I was made temporary Lieutenant over my trips to England as I really only spent time enjoying myself and relaxing, but on one occasion I returned by passenger ship and was the only passenger on it. It seems the ship had been damaged in the Manchester Ship Canal and all the other passengers had been transferred to other ships. Her repairs were quickly made and so I was allowed to join the ship and I steamed to India in grand isolation. The trouble with being in command meant that I got the red tape and paperwork and the worst office to deal with was the pay department. Much of the bumf manufactured in this office was pure obstruction. After any campaign, committees, known as family pension committees, were appointed to identify claimants to pensions, who were fathers or mothers of soldiers killed in action. I was appointed President of one such committee. Some of the claimants had walked three hundred miles across the desert in order to attend. Mostly these people were poor and illiterate folk. I took their fingerprints by way of a signature and I say so myself, these prints were really quite good. Wait for it! Back came the finger prints from the pay office with a letter saying they would have to be taken again. I sat on these letters for ten days and then sent them back with a covering letter saying I now have the honour to forward a new set of fingerprints, which I hoped would be satisfactory. They were accepted!

Peshawar October 1903
Officers 15th Sikhs. Colonel Rowcroft seated centre

Sikh Brigade Officers at Rawalpindi. December 1905
Colonel G. Rowcroft DSO wearing blue patrols seated centre

We were ordered to go to the Mulakund, which had now developed into a frontier station. We were allowed a certain number of tents. I found that we did not require so many and thought I could save the Government some money. I was promptly told that the tentage and been worked out and that I was to take that which had been supplied, or I was to have none at all. Needless to say, reams of correspondence followed. Red tape did not end there. HQ sent me a letter marked secret. This was from the Commander in Chief's office at Simla. "Have you got your mobilisation mules?" I may mention in passing that we were always mobilised at Ferozepore, and ready to go off at once anywhere.

Everyman jack, and every coolly, in the bazaar knew that we had our mobilisation mules, and to pretend any secrecy about it was futile. Letters marked secret were a nuisance. Each had to be kept, recorded, replied to, a copy of the reply made, registered, etc, all by the C.O. himself. Or, another Officer might be detailed to help. To get another Officer up from a mile away, write a rough copy of an answer for him to copy, or dictate a reply to him, was more trouble that it was worth, so I did it myself. I wrote a report complaining that there was no secrecy in the letter concerning the mules. I got a reply, which said, "its all part of the system". I thought, it's a rotten system.

General Denning was appointed to look into Army paperwork. He told me himself that by the time he had finished deleting and abolishing certain redundant army forms, the powers that be, had issued three times as many new ones to replace the ones he had got rid of. A Commanding Officer I know had to visit some of his men and was allowed travelling money. When he sent in his claim a reply came back that his journey, as the crow flies, was ten miles and not the fifteen miles he had asked to be paid for. He simply replied that he rode a horse and now a crow. I believe that the clerks in the pay department were paid for every error they could discover. In addition to our mules, we also had camels. I used to inspect these every day. Normal camels when they are seated fold their four legs in front of them but one I noticed had the strange habit of leaving a front limb stretched right out in the sand. The driver told me there was nothing wrong with it, I inspected it closely and found it had a deep hole in the knee and the driver used to make up a paste of camel hair coloured mud and plugged the hole with it. I told him off and saw that the camel was properly treated.

As I left the camel lines, I noticed a dense dust cloud approaching from the north. When it reached us I discovered it was a swarm of greenfly, millions of them. Where they had come from or where they went I could not say. We were also visited by locusts. Nasty beasts. They devoured everything; I could actually hear their jaws crunching all the available greenery. Local trains used to squash thousands of them on the tracks and the wheels could not get a grip and the trains would come to a stop.

Another of my duties was to preside over a hearing to decide on who was responsible for damaging a sword bayonet. We had a big arsenal and this contained hundreds of these sword bayonets. An artillery man said he was cleaning one and it just bent. He further added that they were all the same. I tried one and found his statement to be true. It was as if they had been made from lead. These were the weapons our lads were given to fight with. My committee reported that these German made bayonets were utterly useless.

Peshawar

In March 1902, we marched to Peshawar. Whoops! I keep forgetting, the fact is I'm getting old and even more stupid! My only excuse is that I'm 86 years of age and I am writing this without a diary or any other notes to help me. Forgive me.

Travelling to Peshawar once with my family, the train suddenly started shaking and threw my two children out of their bunks, and seemed on the point of leaving the rails. We had travelled through an earthquake. Peshawar was noted for its thieves and everyone had to keep a Chowkidar, or watchman. It was largely, blackmail as the watchman was usually one of the gang of thieves, but if you employed him he kept the others away. Each watchman had to deposit a sum of 200 Rupees, this was forfeited if the house was burgled. I lost all my saddlery from my stable one dark night. Our C.O. and the second in command, years previously, had shared a house together, the second pooh-poohed having a watchman. One night returning from a mess dinner he discovered his half of the bungalow had been cleaned out, even the matting on the floors! The watchman on the other side of the house had seen and heard nothing. These watchmen were armed and I heard that one had shot a burglar, assaulted his master and run away. He had to do this as the dead man's family would initiate a blood feud and his life would not be worth much unless he headed for the border. In those days I liked a drink, but did not abuse it. I would have a small peg of whisky at dinner; otherwise I drank soda water, or lemonade. On this day, however, I had had an exhausting afternoon, and on retiring to the Mess got the Indian Mess Sergeant to bring me a whisky, and I took a sip. "What's this, there's no whisky in this!" He replied "yes, Sahib, I poured it out of the whisky bottle myself". He showed me the bottle, I took a sniff at the neck of the bottle and said "this is not whisky, he replied "Oh, Sahib, I have just been to the Doctors and he gave me a bottle of eye-wash". Needless to say, I recovered. At this period I had not had any leave for two years and so I took myself off to

Burma for three months' holiday. I told you my memory was going, but I have just found a diary from which I extract the following items. Stopped at a Dak bungalow where I had breakfast, the slat pot had no spoon, the pepper was in another antediluvian salt cellar of a different pattern. The butter, without a knife, was in a saucer. A dirty tablecloth covered freely with the stains of mustard, tea, gravy and other stains of dubious origins and a table napkin which had been used by all cummers for the last month or so.

On my travels I really enjoyed meeting new people, particularly educated Indians. I met a young man of about 21 dressed in English clothes who spoke to me about the idiot children of Gujerat, to which place he was going. He told me that Indian couples without children prayed to a Saint called, Shah Daula, asking for a child. If their prayers were answered and a son was born to them, the baby would be devoted to the saint. This meant that iron rings would be fixed on the baby's head and its skull would be deformed, the unfortunate child will then be known as one of, Shah Daula's mice. Not so common now, he told me the practice was still occurring, but as of writing this, 1948, I do not know if it would be still allowed. I remember seeing one of these poor creatures in 1927, quite idiotic and helpless, being lead about by the hand. Some Indians are very educated and others are not, I suppose like Society everywhere, it takes all kinds and I seem to get the stranger ones as my personal servants.

I suspected that my Man was doing something with my toothbrush, as it appeared to have a very battered and dirty appearance. After I challenged him he confessed that he cleaned my webbing and my medals with it. Mind you, some of our Europeans could be just as stupid. At Nowshera, an Officer had his horse stolen. Quite how the thief had managed to get it out of the stable was a bit of a mystery so when they caught the man and recovered the horse the Officer said to him, "How on earth did you get the horse out of the stable?" The man said "Sahib, if the constables release me and you give me the horse, I will show you". He was released and given the horse, whereupon he jumped on the horse's back, gave a kick with his heels shouting over his shoulder, as he left the scene, "Cheerio Sahib". Smart fellow!

One afternoon my bearer shouted into my office that the fire alarm had sounded. The fire was in the supply and transport store depot. This had been caused by a Sepoy wondering how much rum was left in a large rum barrel. He struck a match to enable him to see to the bottom of the barrel and the fumes ignited blowing the roof off the storehouse and causing a bang that could be heard for a mile. The two men in the store had to be taken to hospital. It was a wonder that they weren't killed. The same sort of behaviour seems to affect people and strange things happen. I was once on a train and looking out of the window saw that the driver, who could not see around the next bend, was leaning out of his cab blowing a whistle. A minute or two later we had a head on collision with another train. Luckily, there were no injuries, but why the man had not stopped the train prior to the crash I do not know!

Burma

With all my chatter, hopping about with my memories I really should get back to relating my trip to Burma. The sea passage there was rough. The Captain said the roughest they had had that year. In Rangoon I visited the Shway Dragon Pagoda. This was perfectly lovely. The entrance is up numerous steps via a little bazaar, where flowers and little decorated wax candles were sold for leaving at the various shrines. The main pagoda is very high and covered all over with gold. The place is decorated with many statues of Buddah. I thought the whole place looked like fairyland, but shortly after my visit a tiger walked into the pagoda and had to be shot. The Burmese are inveterate smokers. Children who can barely toddle wander about with big cigars in their mouths and the women suck back on cigars the size of rolly polly puddings at least a foot long and they looked absurd. I also saw an example of Chinese foot binding. A little old lady, with the smallest feet I have ever seen, was hobbling along with the aid of a stick.

The weather was hot and humid and I found the mosquitoes at night very trying. I have never lost my appeal to them and I even get them into my nostrils, but they seem to go with the coming of daylight. As we made our way by train up country, vendors at the stations sold cooked prawns, or were they crayfish? They were about 8 inches long and two with bread and butter would make a decent meal.

Further north I took to the road, accompanied by a mysterious bird which I never got a glimpse of, but it seemed to follow me through the trees by the side of the road. It's call, sounded like "How annoying you are", it seemed to follow me for at least two days, but I suppose it was really a succession of the same kind of bird.

The next days march to Yenabin, almost all up hill. It poured with rain and I was soaked, likewise exhausted, and at the rest bungalow I fell into a chair and would have slept had it not been for the mosquitoes. The cart with my baggage did not arrive for two hours. My servant said the carter had been ill. As per usual the insects in these places were numerous. Ants were in the sugar bowl and I took eleven out of my first cup of tea, eight out of the second, and I forget how many from the third. However, the trees and flowers were beautiful. The monkeys in the trees were constantly entertaining and sometimes kicked up an awful rumpus. I found walking in the heat during the monsoon most tiring. On one occasion I bought six plantains from a native, and found these to be the sweetest I had ever tasted. I was advised that Toucan made good eating and so I shot one. This was like eating boiled leather and the soup made from it tasted like hot water in which feathers had been boiled. My servant put the bird's head on the table as I was eating. I objected. The next morning at 7am I had the remains of the bird for breakfast, but black ants had taken up residence in the carcass overnight, so I quickly threw it away.

At the next rest house, there were some native children who took one look at me and bolted. Later on as they peered at me from a distance and I smiled at them, they came closer. I showed them my shikari knife, which pleased them very much, and then my butterfly collection. They stared at them as if they had never seen butterflies before. The next day I got soaking wet again. I took off my clothes at the rest house and rung them out and then put them on again. For several days running, I had been wet and my toes and feet began to suffer and I could not get my boots on whilst wearing thick socks and so had to change to thinner ones. On the third morning, when I awoke, my right eye was closed and my lips were swollen. I had been handling a mauve coloured bean and I was told that it had caused the swelling. There were also plenty of poisonous spiders around, but I managed not to get bitten. A forest officer told me that on one tree alone, he had found five different kinds of spider new to science.

One spider spins a web with what looks like a Maltese cross radiating from the centre. The spider sits in the centre with its legs resting on the arms of the cross so that it can feel any vibration in the web.

My next rest stop was at Hlaingdet after a very hot march. I arrived at midday. At about 3.30, the usual heavy rain having come on at about 3pm. I found an Englishman already there, who had naturally secured the only room with a bed in it, so I had to sleep on the floor. There was another bed, but it had no bottom to it.

I returned to India in the S.S. Madur and was eaten alive by mosquitoes the first night. I was told the ship had just been four months in dock, undergoing repairs and had got so full of mosquitoes that even the dock labourers went on strike and refused to go below decks. The insects eagerly awaited my arrival!

Delhi Durbar

I re-joined my regiment at Peshawar and was ordered with them to Delhi, to take part in some of the stiffest manoeuvres I had ever been in and then afterwards, to take part in Lord Curzon's big Coronation Durbar.

This was a brilliant spectacle. Lord Curzon did not do things by halves! We left Peshawar on the 23rd October 1902, returning on the 19th January 1903. There were, of course, big parades and march-pasts and various other functions and displays. Various Indian Princes' retainers marched around the arena, in all sorts of wonderful costumes and uniforms. Some of them were even in chain-mail armour. The Rajah of Kashmir's lot had two giants in the retinue. One was at least eight feet six inches high, the other slightly shorter. They were strange, hardly human looking beings. All Officers were invited to these functions which used to take place in the afternoon.

Lord Kitchener had just arrived in India as Commander-in-Chief and I received a message that he was to come to my tent and pay me a visit as I was the Commanding Officer of the Fifteenth Sikhs. He arrived with Lord Birdwood who was his Military Secretary and entered my tent, which was sparsely furnished. I had a camp bed, and a camp chair, and a wooden box. One of us had to sit on the box. Lord Kitchener was very pleasant and informative, and related to me his immediate plans. Suddenly, he turned to General Birdwood who had been sitting quietly listening to all that was said, and exclaimed, "I say Birdwood, why are you telling Rowcroft all this? This is all confidential". We both smiled. General Birdwood, hadn't said a word!.

I received an order to parade the regiment for inspection by the Duke of Connaught. Some years before the Duke had dinned with us at our Mess. He got a little mixed up with his memory concerning Sikh regiments, and kept making mistakes, which I pointed out to him. Tut Tut! Royalty must not be corrected!

There were a lot of cavalry regiments, there and one was likely to encounter horseman everywhere. I was galloping back to town on a narrow path when I passed an Indian Cavalryman galloping towards me, our right knees met with a bump and it broke one of the horn buttons of my breeches in two. I turned in the saddle, and was distressed to find I had knocked the man off his horse. He was picking up and re-winding his turban.

The Frontier, Fort Lockhart

After the Durbar in March 1904 we marched to Fort Lockhart on the frontier. This place was right on the edge! One of our piquets, Crag Piquet, was on the edge of a deep precipice overlooking a valley far below, and no one had the slightest inkling of what might be going on in the country beyond! The first intimation anyone would have of an incursion into India from that direction would have been to spy them coming from the Crag Piquet.

Here one constantly lived prepared for anything. Food, water, etc being continually stored as if we expected a siege.

The little fort of Saragurhi, occupied by a party from the 14th Sikhs had been surrounded by tribesmen a few days before we got there. Every one of the Sikhs had been killed. Stepping outside of our fortress we had armed sentries with us, even on the little sports ground we had close to the fort. In the winter we had snow, and in the summer it was very hot. Our mules were either tethered in the snow in the winter, or climbing up and down the hill in the summer, in order to reach a stream from which they could drink. The poor beasts must have had a hard time of it. At the foot of the hills, past Hungoo ran a narrow gauge railway leading in those days to Tull, where we had an outpost, ten or twenty miles away. The railway station there was built like a fort. The train used to crawl along and third class passengers would jump out, pull up a few turnips from the fields alongside and jump back on the train. I heard that the train driver dripped his shovel and jumped down to retrieve it. Colonel Burn, the C.O. of a Dogra regiment, a friend of mine, used to communicate with me by letter. He was some distance from me away in the hills at a place called Takht. I. Suleiman's (Soloman's Throne). A range of hills fifty miles away. Together we decided to attempt contact by heliograph. At a prefixed hour our signallers directed mirrors on what we thought must be the right spot. Presently from the far distance like a little star, appeared from the mountainside and we had joined up! Messages followed and both of us were greatly pleased.

Canada

Whilst still at Fort Lockhart, I went on a year's leave to Canada via the Pacific. The war between Russia and Japan was in progress, and when we got to Tokyo we had to be escorted through a minefield. Whilst passing across the Pacific on the 4th May it was my birthday. Since we crossed the dateline the very next day was the 4th May again so I had another birthday! I got off the ship at Victoria, the capital of British Columbia, in Vancouver Island. Many people whose geography is a bit hazy are confused about Vancouver. Vancouver city is on the main land and the terminus of the transcontinental railway, a very go ahead city. Vancouver Island is a hundred miles away. I was very taken with the country, and decided to settle there when I retired, being so far to the west there was practically no white labour obtainable, and the excellent Chinese were very largely employed. These were reliable and very hard working fellows. The Government, however, in my humble opinion, made two mistakes. The first was, they allowed them to buy land. British immigrants landing at Montreal or Quebec used to take up jobs at those places, or at others as they headed west, and only about one in a hundred ever reached Victoria, mistake no. 2, the Government then stopped all Chinese, Japanese, or Indian labour from entering. The result was the price of wages went up six times what it had been, or often couldn't get labour at all. I had bought a piece of land and looked forward to returning to it.

Ferozepore and Retirement

From Fort Lockhart I marched the regiment back to Ferozepore. I was marching on foot across the bridge over the Sutlej. My Adjutant suddenly called out to the men to break step as the bridge had begun to vibrate. The river, I noticed was flowing backwards. It was the tail end of the Dhurumsala earthquake, when so many of the Gurkha regiments stationed there were killed. We reached Ferozepore an hour later and I could see the earthquake damage on the buildings. Ferozepore was as dusty as ever and I was so worried that another season there would turn me blind. My eyelids had to be treated with sulphate of copper crystal, rather unpleasant. The M.O. gave me some eye drops buy they burnt like fire and blisters formed on my eye balls, preventing me from actually closing my eyes. I sent for the M.O. and he took one sniff from the bottle of drops and he hurled the bottle into the bushes. I never did find out what it was.

In November 1906 I went to England on a year's retirement leave. It was an enormous wrench. Several of the fine Officers I left behind greatly distinguished themselves in the Great War eight years later, while others were killed. (Editor's note: This amazing man later qualified as a surgeon and re-enlisted).

Canada, Hard Work

I thought I would find a knowledge of engineering useful as a settler in Canada so I went to the London Polytechnic and was allowed to undergo a sort of condensed course, which I found very interesting. I didn't stay long in England and soon took off on the boat for Canada. At sea I overheard a conversation which amused me. It went like this, 'the man sharing my cabin with me has his little ways. He's only got one brush. First he cleans his boots with, then his clothes, and then he brushes his hair with it, well after all if you've only got one brush in the world!' Arrived at Victoria, we stayed at a hotel, and my son and I would start off after breakfast to work on my land. Although it was only a mile and a half from the centre of Victoria, it looked as though it was in the heart of the country. This was because a little range of high ground covered with fir trees intervened, the lower part of the hill belong to me, I became an expert with an axe and felled several trees for fencing. Strenuous work followed. I bought plenty of tools and we built a shack with several rooms in it and then filled it with furniture. The work was really hard and for a while I used to go to bed every night with every bone and muscle in my body aching. After a while I got so tough I felt nothing.

I planted fruit trees; apples, pears, plums etc and they did well. I also bought a cart and a buggy and a very nice little horse. This was indispensable, for visits to Victoria for shopping but it made extra work. My son took up an appointment with the Montreal Bank in Victoria. (Editor's note: This son is, Maurice Rowcroft, later a Lt Colonel in the Indian Army). An excellent China man was engaged to assist me. The land was mostly on a slope and we drained the part in front and the garden and orchard with earthen pipes. I soon got a notice to fence in the whole of my land, this required scores of cedar posts and quantities of heavy galvanized wire netting. I built quite a respectable sized barn. On one side was the buggy shed, on the other a workshop, and in the centre a fuel store and a place for odds and ends, with a hayloft above. This was all of wood. Window frames I bought ready made. All the rest I did with my own hands. I made the sides flat on the ground and raised them up into position. I harvested a crop of oats, which a neighbour bought, and cut hay, part of which was stacked and part stowed in the barn. I lived in the barn for sometime and then built a decent house like all the others.

The climate at Victoria itself is on the whole very dry. From about April until September there is not a drop of rain, yet if one looked towards Sooke, only six miles away one saw heavy rain frequently falling.

The winters, on the whole were mild but, without the least warning, the temperature would go below zero and everything froze solid. The meat, the bread and the butter all frozen hard. I took a kettle of hot water off the kitchen range and poured it on the stone steps outside. It turned to ice as it hit the stone. In building the house, I had seen that all the pipes were get.at.able, not hidden in the walls. Needless to say every pipe burst. The mains pipe was a quarter of a mile away and I laid down an iron pipe underground, crossing the main road, and buried fairly deeply so that it did not freeze. What made these cold snaps worse was a fierce wind from the pacific, towards which my land slopped, this made the cold more intense.

The Government made life extremely difficult with their rules and regulations. I found a notice tacked to a tree near my house directing me to spray all my fruit trees, the notice threatened that if I did not do this within ten days men will be sent to do it and I would be charged. There were plenty of good fruit tree sprays on sale but they wanted local farmers to use an obscure and expensive spray. It was obvious that someone in power would soon have plenty of extra money in their pockets. This was not the only instance of this kind of graft, and together with labour problems and an enormous hike in wages to obtain it; this was the last straw as far as I was concerned. I had imagined a life of relaxation and fishing which I was fond of, but the never ending hard work and official interference made it impossible. I put the property on the market. There was a slight boom on, and I sold immediately. I heard that the person who bought it from me sold it on again that same day for a thousand dollars more than he paid me.

Dr Rowcroft

Back once more to dear old England, and I began to think of a medical career again. My Army examination was accepted instead of the usual entrance exam and I joined up at St Bartholomew's (Barts) I did my five years there and passed first in anatomy and second or third in all the other subjects. (If I don't sing my own praises who will?). As soon as I had qualified the First World War broke out. I applied to the War Office for an Infantry job. Nothing doing. There was a black mark against my name for the objections I used to raise against frivolous matters. I wrote again and pointed out that I was now qualified as a medical man. I was soon given an appointment as a Major in the Indian Medical Service and I was ordered to report to Barton-on-Sea in Hampshire where there was a big hospital for sick and wounded Indians.

I soon found I was idling my time here, and applied for a job on a hospital ship and was very soon appointed to the Glengorm Castle. This I much enjoyed. As I have said before and my memory is not what it was, I am very old but whilst on the Glengorm Castle I did keep a diary of sorts in the shape of letters sent home, and these I have unearthed. Some of the contents may be of interest. The ship used to make voyages to various Ports, conveying sick and wounded, sometimes to Alexandria with Indians to carry on their homeward journey and bringing back British sick and wounded. Sometimes we went to Marseilles. Our Sister ship was blown up by a mine at Boulogne. My Commanding Officer was Lt. Colonel Prall of the I.M.S., who had previously spent thirteen years as principal Medical Officer at Aden, and appeared to have enjoyed it. Water was scarce there and he did not use soap in his bath water as the water was saved for his horse to drink.

On the 30th September 1915 on Boulogne we took on 602 cases of sick and wounded Indians. We were very tightly packed and every cot was filled and scores of others had to be laid on the decks, the mattresses touching. Moans and groans were very audible, but all without exception were very plucky, and underwent painful dressings without a flinch or sound. We got them off the next day at Southampton, three train loads.

Lt. Colonel Maurice Rowcroft (Retd)
Royal Indian Army Service Corp.
(carrying the stick he has needed since being wounded
in the First World War) alongside his sister Ruby.
Household servants pose on the steps behind taken at
Coonoor in the Nilgiri Hills.

Two days later I heard that my eldest son, Maurice, who had joined up with the Canadians, and then been given a Commission in the Lincolns, had been badly wounded at Loos. He was shot through the body, the bullet also injured the hip joint and for many years when he bent his thigh it used to make the most extraordinary sound, but he said it didn't hurt. He became an A1 tennis player, and runner up, some years later, of the English Championship. (According to onlookers he actually won, the deciding ball he played given as out by the Umpire, those with a better view declared it was, in fact, 'in'. Having recovered he was sent back to France and was again severely wounded in the opening battle of the Somme, his left arm shattered above the elbow. In this condition, while going back to his lines, he stopped to help dig out a man who had been buried by soil thrown up by a shell, which I thought was very fine of him. The surgeons debated whether to take his arm off, but it recovered and was then 2 inches shorter than the other arm.

Getting back to my hospital ship, we were anchored off Cowes, in the Isle of Wight. I went ashore and was quietly reading in the club when a naval officer came in and asked if any of us were on the Glengorm Castle. He told me that a number of Indians were drunk and fighting on the road near the pier and would I please restore law and order and remove them to the ship. I went and saw that there was no end of a row going on, and the blood was flowing freely. I managed to get hold of a few men of the 88th Carnatic Infantry, (the Guard of the Ship). Together we arrested the men at the centre of this disturbance and had them taken back aboard by a tug boat of the Naval Transport Service. (Editor's note: I was told by family members that when Surgeon Major Rowcroft dealt with these men's' black eyes and split lips the following morning he was not very sympathetic, and no doubt relished applying liberal doses of iodine.

Another trip to Boulogne, and then we were ordered to Marseilles with several hundred Indians to be landed there, and then on to Alex with a number of cripples to be sent back to India. Amongst the latter were four lunatics in my charge. On another trip I had 23. The C.O. seemed to think birds of a feather flock together. I had a mild tussle with one of them. He had not spoken a word since he came on board but that day whilst I visited him in a padded cell, he said to me "I want to go", so leading him by his arm I took him into the ward but he wanted to go up on deck and I stopped him. It took four of us to get him back in his cell. (Most of these men were probably shell shocked but that illness was not yet recognized).

We had some very rough weather, but I was not seasick. I suppose the number of gales we encountered was normal, but we seemed to be forever getting into them. At Alex on one occasion, about half a dozen ships were blown from their moorings, but we held firm. On the 8th November we reached England again and passing through the boom I noticed a tug at anchor, marking the spot where one of our ships had been blown up two days before. Two torpedo boats dashed out of harbour and spotted two German submarines, sank one and rounded the other up, brand new and only eight hours out from Kiel. On the 13th September, I operated on a man who had been wounded at Gallipoli. I took an iron disk out of his leg that had obviously been punched from a quarter inch thick plate to make a hole for a rivet. The Turks were using them as shrapnel. Two days later I was rushed to one of my cases he was bleeding badly. He had a terrible wound across his back caused by an enormous piece of metal. It looked as if a gigantic cheese scoop had dug a deep furrow in his flesh. The left shoulder blade had part of it carried away with a lot of muscle. The day before, a piece of shoulder blade had come away while being dressed. I had applied skin grafts a few days before, and all was doing well. He was now bleeding badly, but I managed to get it under control and in the end he recovered. Back and forth to Boulogne we went, continually on the look out for mines. These were laid by German submarines, some of them in the harbour itself, I saw many explode and ships blown up by them. Because of this danger we had to wear lifebelts, but reached England safely and started off for Marseilles again, tremendous amount of rolling in the Bay of Biscay, 12 hours in Marseilles loading the wounded and off back to England. We seemed doomed to encounter storms and I saw a wave come over the side and knocked a steward off his feet, the tea tray he was carrying went flying. Back to Alex, discharged our wounded and back to Marseilles. Took on 140 and started back to Alex. En route we picked up a wireless call for help from a Dutch steamer, she had been torpedoed and we assisted her.

I again wrote to the War Office offering my services as an Infantry Officer, but I received no reply. I had assumed that with so many Officers killed there would be a place for me. (At this time, George was 54 years old). On each voyage we always had lifeboat drill and the more able patients were detailed to help the badly wounded in the event of an emergency. I told two Indians that in an emergency they were to go to Mr So and So's bed and assist him up on deck, they appeared not to understand me. Up comes the Indian Sub-Assistant Surgeon and puts it to them another way. "When the ship starts sinking you two are to help Mr So and So up on deck". They quite understood. Among our sick and wounded was a young fellow who with his platoon was attacked by a Squadron of the Deaths' Head German Hussars at Mons. He had his foot broken by a horse and he also had two ribs broken. After that he was gassed, and then sent home with a weak heart. I had another man who was stabbed by a Turk's bayonet from the front, whilst another Turk stabbed him in the back. He recovered. He bayoneted and killed the man in front of him and a comrade shot the one who stabbed him in the back. I had another patient who had gone deaf and dumb. One night in the ward, he dreamt that he was being chased by Turks and shouted for help and woke himself up and found he could hear and speak once more. Another man had a shell burst near him and caused his eyelids to go into a spasm, although not blind, he couldn't open his eyes to see. One day he was standing by the ship's bell, which was rung to sound the hour. This made him jump; he opened his eyes and could see.

Hospitals

Back in England, I went to the War Office and asked if any reply had been sent to my letter. My file was sent for and a man bought in a mass of paperwork done up in a cover. The cover was opened and there on top was a letter, which was supposed to have been sent to me. I had better not say how I felt. I was not given the letter to read, but I was told I would have the first regimental command vacancy that occurred. I was advised to leave the Glengorm Castle and proceed to a large hospital for the wounded at Millbank so as to be ready to join a regiment at once. At the hospital there were some Indians and my linguistic capabilities were made use of. I was also given a ward of British lads. Days passed and nothing happened, when I met an old comrade back from France. He said I didn't have the faintest chance of getting an appointment and he explained why. So many regiments had been wiped out in France, leaving so many C.O.s stranded, they were all promised regiments before any newcomer would be considered, and I had left the Glengorm Castle! The Indian wounded were all dealt with until there were none left at Millbank and my temporary appointment had expired. They offered me a job in the Royal Army Medical Corp. I was advised that this would leave me standing idle for a lot of the time so I declined the offer and went into private practice. I thought I would be more use to the community as a Doctor than standing around in Khaki. I very soon got an appointment as Medical Officer in Charge of a hospital for sick and wounded at Hampstead. This was financed by a wealthy American, they had not entered the war yet. I served here for sometime but inefficiency in the management was rife and I reported the fact to the American gentleman and asked him for it to be put right. He would not budge on this matter, so I said, goodbye. Moorfield Eye Hospital snapped me up and I became third House Surgeon. In the back of my mind I could see my return to India and so decided to acquire useful experience, which I knew, would be required in the tropics and to that end I worked in several 'Special' hospitals. At about this time the Germans began bombing London using airships and I think I was beneath every raid that occurred. If I remember right the first bomb was dropped at night by aeroplane and it landed on Victoria Station. Aeroplanes used to come over in one's and two's, later in greater numbers. Moorfields' Hospital and a Cocoa factory were all in one big building with a dividing wall between them. The factory had some heavy machinery, which made violent thuds and bangs. I was operating on a lady's eye one day when the bangs started and got louder and louder. I looked out of the window behind me and saw a flight of German aeroplanes, about thirty-five of them coming straight towards us dropping bombs. Our shrapnel appeared to be bursting in the middle of them, but without bringing one down. I went down to the hall where the patients who had seen what was coming, the hall had a glass roof, were rushing about and making a great row. There were many foreigners amongst them, and they seemed the most scared and noisy. The aeroplanes soon passed over. They stopped dropping bombs just before the hospital, but resumed a little way beyond. It was God's mercy, for they would not have known it as a hospital. Within a few minutes wounded folk began coming in for treatment and for a little while we functioned as a General Hospital. One man came in with a terrible wound on his face and I thought he had lost an eye, but on cleaning him up I realised his eye was uninjured. As soon as duty permitted I went up to inspect the damage. The street leading away from the front of the hospital was severely damaged on the left hand side with some house fronts blown out with their room contents exposed to view. At Moorfields I developed my skill and after some months there I received an invitation to become House Surgeon at the Royal Ear Nose and Throat Hospital in Gray's Inn Road. Another good opportunity for me to absorb special knowledge.

Air raids continue and the women in our big ward used to be terrified. The Matron was very brave. She and I used to sit in the women's ward during air raids to encourage the poor patients. Those who were able climbed under their beds, feeling safer there. I used to read a medical book and pretended to be unconcerned. Our guns were firing away too, so there was quite a racket. A plane was flying towards the hospital dropping bombs as it came, one, two, three, four, five, each one louder than the last. No. 6 would have caught us but never came! In the next room Matron picked up a piece of shrapnel. All the windows in the house next door were broken, and a horse was lying dead in the stable. Tramlines were cut as if they were made of soft butter. I subsequently worked at two other hospitals, one of them for women and children in Shadwell. When air raids began we would carry the women on their mattresses down into the basement. (Editor's note: I checked with Moorfield Hospital and the Museum of London. The former replied that the Operating Theatre had been on the third floor overlooking City Road, and the Museum confirmed that air raids had taken place at that time).

Back to India

At the 11th hour of the 11th day of the 11th month of 1918, the 'Cease Fire' sounded and the First Great War ended. We returned to India, and we went to Bareilly. I made friends with an Afghan Prince who was exiled. He asked me to look at his young son, four years of age. I found he was suffering from tonsils and adenoids. He asked me to operate and I had to administer the chloroform and do the operation unaided, and it was quite successful. He rather shocked me by taking away the tonsils and adenoids on a white china plate to show his mother.

We somehow drifted to Saharandur in the United Provinces. Like other places in India we had problems in that place with insects. The termites were very bad. I had a small dog who used to take a great delight in eating them, disgusting beast.

By this time I had developed a habit of shouting at my servants, not necessarily with any evil intent, but it was bought home to me in an amusing way. I had a very excellent middle-aged bearer, and the following conversation was one day overheard. My wife's ayah said to my bearer "are you not afraid when the Sahib speaks so loudly to you!" My bearer replied, "good grief, no I've served in the Artillery!" Loud noises had no terrors for him as he was practically deaf and I was tickled to find my speech placed on the level of gunfire.

The six monthly upheavals from the heat of the planes to the cool of the hill stations has many disadvantages and is most expensive. Wealthy folks have two houses, one in the planes and one in the hills. After a few years we decided to move homes again.

Palestine

We stayed in a hotel for a month at Portside and then moved to Jaffa. The approach to the town from the sea is very picturesque. There was no real harbour so ships had to lie at anchor some way off and goods and passengers went ashore in boats. The house of Simon the Tanner, where St. Peter stayed, is still pointed out. Arab porters are very strong and can carry one's belongings with ease. I once saw four Indian soldiers struggle to carry a packing case, which an Arab shouldered with no trouble at all. I even saw an Arab porter carrying an enormous case on his back. I enquired what was in it and found it to be a piano. If there's a really big case a second Arab will share the load, not actually lifting it but walking along side murmuring encouragement. I wondered what would happen if a porter tripped! He would be converted into a pancake on the spot! The women dressed from head to foot in black, which must be very well in the cool weather, but this dress must be very trying in the heat. I noticed most of them wear high heels, regular stilts, even the small girls. Many of them wear gold and silver coins about their faces and some of them have their faces tattooed, it doesn't make them look very attractive. Sometimes the whole chin and lower lip is tattooed black and they look repulsive.

Blindness is common and the causes are dirt, apathy, and negligence. I have seen children with a dozen flies crawling around their eyes, and they don't seem to bother to brush them away. Flies, indeed are an absolute plague, especially in the summer, and there are many species, including biting ones which are as bad as mosquitoes. Sand flies are legion.

Donkeys and camels are the beast of burden and an Indian camel would have a nasty shock if he were transferred to the ownership of an Arab. Indian transport regulations state that the pace of a camel is 2 miles an hour. I would say that Palestinian camels rush along at 5 miles an hour, and the beast is almost trotting. The nose-peg isn't used, as in India, but a headstall, and a cruel one it is. The noseband on each side where it crosses the edge of the jaw has a small iron plate in it and this cuts into the jaw and large sores develop.

Donkeys, usually white ones, are ridden by the well-to-do. To make the gentleman feel he is riding a big horse an enormous saddle is used and the donkey is steered with a cane or stick striking one side of its neck or the other. To come to a halt, he hisses at it and the docile beast obeys. If not, it is beaten. No one prevents this cruelty and as I did not know the language I was unable to do so myself.

Chickens are bought in for sale from the surrounding villages to Jaffa in hundreds every day. They are tied in bunches and strapped on to the side of a donkey and must suffer as they jig jog into town. No attempt to inculcate kindness enters the heads of the educated. I spoke to an English-speaking lady about it and she curtly replied that she had never seen any cruelty.

A strange thing I noticed about Jaffa was the number of horseshoes to be found in the streets. The price of iron was high and yet one could collect a ton of horseshoes in quite a short time. The shoes often looked new and the Siths must have done quite a good trade. This place is famous for its oranges and they have rather a pleasant custom. At the first and last consignments from each orchard, the camels carrying them are dressed in gaily-coloured silks, beads, bells, tassels and trimmings. They make for quite a sight, jingling along as they bustle by.

Grapes are in quite good supply and I was looking over a piece of wasteland with a few dry sticks on it. I asked an Arab how much for the land and he gave me a very high price. I was, in fact, gazing at a vineyard. The sticks were vines, and being winter, they were leafless. They are not trained, but allowed to grow like bushes, unsupported. I heard that a good kind of grape was grown somewhere further east, but their skins were so thin and delicate that they could not bear transport.

The Pariah dogs are not as bad as the Indian ones and look more wolfish, and I knew of a man being attacked and badly bitten.

Sheep were numerous and less timid than any I have met elsewhere, and did not seem to be frightened by dogs.

For six months we stayed at the ancient town of Lydda, in a wooden house made chiefly of packing cases nailed into studding.

Malta

A year of Palestine was enough, and we thought we would try Malta. We were told it was a genial spot with a nice climate, which was what we were after. We stayed at a hotel in Alexandria for about a week and on our usual diet of macaroni and tomatoes. We then got a passage on a small German tramp steamer, carrying two or three passengers. The Captain gave up his cabin to us. A German passenger who fought in the War had been shot in the foot and was quite lame. He spoke English and was quite a pleasant fellow.

We got a very grand house at Sliema, a little way from Valetta. It was largely built of white marble with a large staircase leading to the upper floor, enormous rooms, and a tiny garden at the back. There were two grapevines, which produced enormous quantities of excellent green grapes in the summer.

I did a lot of medical work, and at one time took charge of St George's Hospital at Valetta for about a month while the regular man was on leave in England.

We did not find Malta to be what we expected. It gets quite hot in the summer with a hot wind called the Sirocco or the Shiroc blowing in from the Sahara, which quite prostrates many of the people, though we didn't think much of it after the hot winds of India. In the winter it is cold with blustering winds and snow. In the hot weather, sand flies are a nuisance and the glare of the sun off white buildings can be quite trying, and I found I had to use tinted glasses, which I abhor. We visited St Paul's bay where the Saint landed after he was shipwrecked and I had always pictured it as a sandy cove, but it is all rock. No wonder his ship foundered.

Maltese beggars are quite well dressed, and a friend of mine was invited to one of these beggars' daughter's wedding. He decided to go out of kindness and arrived at a large mansion, and was surprised to see the beggar lived like a prince, and the reception went off with great style. It must have cost a fortune – never judge a book by its cover!

Back to India – again

I was looking forward to being back in India, and we boarded a P&O steamer for the gorgeous east once more. Time and time again, I had read of the beauty of the Nilgiri Hills in South India and we decided to try those regions.

We went to Coonoor. Some friends of ours wrote from Bangalore, and inveigled us into going there. They said it had the finest climate in India. I dispute this; it is a day's journey by train from Coonoor. It is about 3000 feet above sea level and this saves it fro really excessive heat, but it was almost always hotter than was comfortable. Mosquitoes of every kind abounded, and there was always a shortage of water. This has since been remedied. I hated the place. My wife, however, liked it because of the shops.

Well, where will we to go next, someone told me Algiers was a good place, so I got a guidebook and studied it. Of course! It was just the place! Why on earth hadn't we heard of it before? So, off to Algiers we went!

We lodged at a boarding house kept by a charming Belgian lady. Well curious as it may seem, Algiers had its drawbacks! For one thing, it was built in tiers on a steep hillside, so walking is rather strenuous. Trains exist, but one does not keep fit sitting around in trains.

In the cold weather the climate was pleasant, but as soon as the sun went down it got very cold, and one required warmer clothing. Chest troubles seem to be the common ailment and I would not go there if I had lung trouble. The summers were nearly as bad as India. Heat, dust storms, hot winds from the Sahara, and mosquitoes. All the French folk who can, and rich Arabs migrate in the summer to the south of France. My daughter Ruby, whose husband was in Canada, now joined us and we all moved once more to Canada, in spite of our experiences twenty years before.

Canada – again

Our destination was Vancouver City. We had been to many places in the world, but not Africa, Australia, or the West Indies. My wife shied off Australia on account of the labour difficulty. As regards Kenya, I had written to a man and he told me the Home Government treated settlers badly, so that put me off. I found that those who praised the place were men with fixed well paid Government jobs. The journey by sea to Canada in an Italian steam ship called the Fella (which was sunk by us in World War II) took us through Sargasso Sea, which I had always pictured as 1 sort of mass of floating seaweed. Actually, we saw very little. We touched one or two W. Indian islands, and then through the Panama Canal. In the Pacific I treated a sick person via wireless. We carried no ship's doctor, but a middle-aged nurse, who used to attend to the cruise minor injuries. The sick man was on a ship three hundred miles away, and I advised them of the correct treatment. I was unable to check on him as communication was interrupted by atmospheric conditions. We made port in Seattle and remained there for four days, and made several interesting visits ashore. I forgot to say that we had also called in at San Francisco and Los Angeles, but not long enough to see much. The oil fields one drove through on shore did not look inviting; a sea of derricks.

We settled in Vancouver City for a while. The winter that followed was not as cold as Vancouver Island, but it was more than cold enough for me, and as my daughter was returning to England we upped sticks again.

Back to Coonoor

This time we sent via the Pacific, in a Japanese ship as far as Tokyo. It was cold, but our cabins were nice and warm. We passed some of the Aleutian Islands and they looked a forbidding sight, covered in snow. In Tokyo, the Japanese were friendly and we were interviewed by newspaper reporters. They took great interest in our dog, as it was somewhat of the sausage dog variety, but much sturdier. She told them how he had travelled round the world and the next morning we found his photo and an article in the local newspaper. From Tokyo, we sailed to Madras in a French ship, held together with thick coats of paint. We survived the trip and reached Madras. Here I bought a motorcar and decided to drive up to Ootacamund in it, sending on our baggage by rail. I got a driver who knew the way and we set off. At Ooty - the Queen of Hill stations - we first stayed at a boarding house, but soon managed to get a house of our own, on rent. It wanted a lot of repairing and I couldn't get the owner to do it. Ooty proved a disappointment. We arrived on the 10th January 1931. It was winter and cold with ice in the puddles on the road. In April it rained, and in May it rained and from then on until the end of December it rained almost every day. We didn't know it at the time but that was a very bad year and Ooty is not usually so moist. We are on the move again, this time to Coonoor, a thousand feet lower. (Editor's note: Here George stopped and made a home. This is where I found his grave in 2002).

The wettest place in India is Cherrapoonjee in Assam, with its seven hundred inches per year. I heard a story once that the local water carrier, whenever he passed the rain gauge and seeing it half-full of water, conveniently filled it up as he passed. The Coonoor climate was good. It is almost like a perpetual spring and summer. Roses and flowers all the year round. How they keep it up I can't imagine. You see a rose bush covered with flowers and they will bloom for weeks, and the flowers will gradually die off. A few weeks later fresh buds and flowers, and the whole process goes on repeating itself continually.

Snow is unknown and frosts are very slight and only appear in deep valleys and low-lying areas where there is no wind. Showers occur now and then, helping to keep everything green and verdant. In the months of March, April and May we have several weeks of dry weather. There is hardly any dust as the roads are tarred. The elevation is between 6,000 to 6,500 feet and being within 11 degrees of the equator, keeps the temperature warm.

The hill stations in the Himalayas do catch extremely cold winters. We do get the monsoons and one is periodically flooded. Ooty gets the southwest monsoon, and Coonoor gets the northeast, the difference being ascribed to a range of mountains. (Editor's note: Coonoor and Ooty are hill stations in the Western Ghats in South India).

My only objection to Coonoor is the Municipal Taxes. One is taxed for everything. I got a booklet from the Council Office, which laid out the list of taxes and came to the conclusion the only thing you could do without being taxed for it was breathing! I think if one of the Councillors caught you breathing harder than usual you would get a bill for air at the end of the month! Apart from the taxes, one can live at Coonoor comfortably all the year round, except for an excess of water in the monsoon.

We have the railway here and this runs from Ooty down to the plains to a place called Metupallayam. There are no foothills to the Nilgiris as they rise abruptly up from the plain. (Editor's note: The rack and pinion light railway still runs. I have used it many times).

There are plenty of big cats about - especially tigers. A truck passed me the other day with two dead tigers in it; either they were shot for sport or they had come too close for comfort. We even had one sunbathing in my son's garden at Coonoor! I admit this is not the usual custom.

Trout have been introduced into local rivers and quite good fishing is to be had. Masheer can be caught in the Bhowani River two or three days march off. A friend caught a record-breaking 54 pound fish there.
I started a small dispensary at Coonoor, and kept it going for a few years.

The Second World War broke out in 1939 and I offered my services in a medical capacity. I was then 78 years old but still pretty fit and used to walk several miles every day. In due time I received a polite official reply saying that if I was wanted they would let me know. A year or so later a frantic appeal for doctors was published. I again applied and in return received an elaborate form of several large pages of questions. How old was I? What were my qualifications? What was my father? What was my caste? And scores of other questions. I had already given this information in my original application and this idiotic red tape disgusted me.

In 1944, my wife died, and as she had been suffering from an incurable complaint, it was a merciful release. I sold my house and teamed up with my daughter who was now living at my son's house. He had retired from the Army but had been asked to re-join. My daughter had done sterling work in putting up Officers on leave (of both sexes), and was almost always full up.

Let me tell you about the snakes we killed in the garden. Rat snakes up to 7ft long were very common. I don't think we get cobras quite so high but there are plenty of Russell's Vipers. Nearby, we have Wellington Golf Course. On the course there is a small copse, which the caddies would not enter to fetch golf balls, as it was full of Russell's Vipers. We also had scorpions. Someone placed a large bunch of flowers on my dressing table and I noticed that there was a scorpion in it - how nice! One fell off a rosebush onto my gardener's neck and stung him, but it didn't seem to worry him much.

My Work with the Medical Mission

I am afraid I was living a rather aimless and useless life and I heard of an independent mission in the wilds of Dehra Dun District of the United Provinces. They required help in their hospital and I wrote offering such medical and evangelical help as I could give. (Editor's note: George Rowcroft had always been quite a religious man and in his later years became a Lay Preacher. There is a plaque to him inside All Saints Church, Coonoor). My offer was gratefully and gladly received. One of the reasons it was difficult for me to treat Indians in Coonoor was the language difficulty. Tamil is mostly spoken along with some Kannadan and Malayallam and Telugu. Most of the Indians in Coonoor can't understand each other and have to resort to the English they learnt at school. It was a relief to be in Dehra Dun and to talk Urdu again. I had forgotten quite a lot.

The hospital work was interesting and a lot of my patients were blind and I was expected to do miracles. A blind woman arrived and said "I want medicine to make me see again". Unfortunately, we did not have that kind of medicine. Treatment was preceded by an Evangelical address and prayers. Some people listened keenly and others completely ignored it. People attending the hospital would be issued with a numbered ticket. A man would come into my surgery and present ticket No. 6, I would tell him to go out and send in the man with No. 1 ticket. In due time No. 1 ticket would arrive at my desk. "Good morning, what's the trouble?" "Eh?" "What's the trouble?" "I've got a pain." "When did it begin?" "It's all up my arm." "When did it begin?" "Oh, five years ago, and I can't see well in my left eye." "When did that begin to trouble you?" "Eh?" "When did that begin to trouble you?" "About four months ago." "Have you had anything done for it?" "Eh?" "Have you had anything done for it?" "No. And I itch all over." (he then began to scratch himself). The patient is examined and a prescription is written. "Get the medicine from the compound and take one tablet three times a day after eating. Not before, or it may give you a pain." "Eh?" I repeated my instructions. "Do you understand? The pharmacist will explain it to you." "Eh?" "Send in the next patient as you go out." "Wait a minute Sahib, I have got this wound on my foot; it's been there for two months and won't get better." I dressed the wound and said "Now send in the next patient." "Eh?"

At this stage, I had better mention my family motto on the crest is 'PATIENTIA'!

Strange cases would come in sometimes, a father brought in his daughter aged two and said she had got a pea stuffed up her nose. I examined her and believe it or not, removed a whole pod. How the child managed to get it up its nose I can't think. Another lady told me she'd got a moth in her ear, and she said it was flying about. She added that she had poured water in her ear but it had not had any effect. I poured a drop or two of soothing oil into her ear. Right away a commotion ensued and something tried to back out of her ear, and with a pair of forceps I managed to remove a very large spider! All's well that ends well. By the 15th May 1946 it had grown hot, and according to custom our mission hospital closed (there is another hospital not far off which remains open).

I have come up to the mountain heights of Mussoorie where the climate is like an English Spring. Yesterday, we had a lovely view of the Eternal Snows much higher and further off. I do not expect to rejoin the hospital, and the dear good friends there. My end cannot be far off and I have certainly had a somewhat wonderful career mercifully protected on many occasions. My guardian angel must come for me and in my case, it won't be long!

I will end this now. Goodbye!

(Ed. George went home to his daughter Ruby's bungalow, Royston, at Coonoor in the beautiful Nilgiri Hills and lived for several years until he died in 1953 aged 91).

Tony and Bridget Pickford listening to me in rapt attention as I describe the graves I am searching for - or perhaps not.
Tiger Hill Cemetery, Coonoor, 2003

Coonoor Railway Station. Next stop Ootacamunde (Ooty)

IN LOVING MEMORY
OF

COLONEL GEORGE FRANCIS ROWCROFT D.S.O
LATE 15TH (LUDHIANA) SIKHS

BORN 4TH MAY 1861
DIED 26TH APRIL 1953
WITH CHRIST - IS FAR BETTER

George Rowcroft's grave. Tiger Hill, Coonoor, S. India

Standing as if transported from the Cotswolds, All Saints Church in the Indian Hill Station of Coonoor.
Inside there is a plaque recording George Francis Rowcroft, regular attendance.
The bungalow in the foreground is the last home of his son, Maurice.

Photo Left: The slate of marble arranged for Maurice.
Tiger Hill, Coonoor, 2003.

Photo Above: Dee and Jim.
Somewhere in South India, 2003.

From Left
Victor Dey. Coffee planter and director of one of South India's best "Homestay" holiday centres.
One of the coffee plantation girls - Kuppamudi Estate, Sultans Battery, Wyanad District, S. India.
One of Victor Dey's tree houses on the estate.

Dee recording what remains 'recordable' at a cemetery in Tellicherry

little.

Thomas Matthew.
My good friend and driver these many years.
No safer man at the wheel on India's hairy roads.
Employed by pioneer travel of Cochin, Kerala, S. India

Tom helping me record a grave epitaph at Mannatoddy, S. India, 2006

The verandah outside my rooms at Victor Dey's holiday centre.

Christian Cemetery, Tellicherry. It looks like a lost cause, but for a small outlay these places can be saved and this is where. The British Association for Cemeteries in South Asia usually help.

THE END